Telling Western Stori

Also by Richard W. Etulain

Author:

Owen Wister
Ernest Haycox
Religion in the Twentieth-Century West: A Bibliography
Re-imagining the Modern American West: A Century of Fiction, History, and Art
The American West—Comparative Perspectives: A Bibliography

Coauthor:

Conversations with Wallace Stegner on History and Literature
The American West: A Twentieth-Century History

Editor:

Jack London on the Road: The Tramp Diary and Other Hobo Writings
The American Literary West
Western Films: A Short History
Writing Western History: Essays on Major Western Historians
Basques of the Pacific Northwest: A Collection of Essays
Contemporary New Mexico 1940–1990
Myths and the American West
Does the Frontier Experience Make America Exceptional?

Coeditor:

Interpretive Approaches to Western American Literature
The Popular Western: Essays Toward a Definition
The Idaho Heritage
Idaho History: A Bibliography
The Frontier and American West
Anglo-American Contributions to Basque Studies
Basque Americans
Fifty Western Writers: A Bio-Bibliographical Guide
A Bibliographical Guide to the Study of Western American Literature
Faith and Imagination: Essays on Evangelicals and Literature
The Twentieth-Century West: Historical Interpretations
Religion and Culture
The American West in the Twentieth Century: A Bibliography
Researching Western History: Topics in the Twentieth Century
Religion in Modern New Mexico
By Grit and Grace: Eleven Women Who Made the American West
Portraits of Basques in the New World
With Badges and Bullets: Lawmen and Outlaws in the Old West

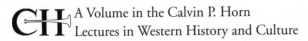 A Volume in the Calvin P. Horn
Lectures in Western History and Culture

Telling Western Stories

From Buffalo Bill to Larry McMurtry

Richard W. Etulain

Albuquerque

The University of New Mexico Press

Library of Congress Cataloging-in-Publication Data

Etulain, Richard W.
Telling western stories : from Buffalo Bill to Larry McMurtry /
Richard W. Etulain — 1st ed.
    p.   cm.   — (Calvin P. Horn lectures in Western history and culture)
Includes bibliographical references (p.   ) and index.
ISBN 0-8263-2139-9 (alk. paper)
ISBN 0-8263-2140-2 (pbk. : alk. paper)
1. American fiction — West (U.S.). — History and criticism. 2. Frontier and
pioneer life in literature. 3. Western stories — History and criticism.
4. Storytelling — West (U.S.). — History. 5. Oral tradition — West (U.S.)
6. West (U.S.) — In literature. I. Title. II. Series
PS374.W4 E93 1999
813.009'3278—dc21   99-6381
                      CIP

For four women:

My grandmother, Jennie Wiley Gillard,
for buying me books and telling stories.

My mother, Mary Gillard Etulain,
for making sure that her sheepranch son got an education.

My wife, Joyce Oldenkamp Etulain,
for being my best supporter for nearly forty years.

My daughter, Jacqueline Etulain Partch,
for delightfully carrying on the tradition of story.

Contents

Illustrations

Preface

WHEN I WAS A BOY, my Basque father often took me to the ranch ranges and to the mountains to check on his bands of sheep. On those trips to the sheepcamps, Dad kept me entertained with story after story. I learned of his Old World beginnings in the fabled Pyrenees Mountains north of Pamplona, Spain, his long trip to the Pacific Northwest, and his earliest sheepherding experiences on the isolated, treacherous hills of central Washington. Usually Dad's tales swept on to tell of saving his money, buying his first land, and beginning his career as a sheepman with his brother.

Alongside my father's stories were my mother's remembrances of her family's experience on the northern sodhouse frontier. In anecdote-filled narratives, she re-called the journeys of her parents from southern Minnesota to the Dakotas and on to the state of Washington during the late nineteenth and early twentieth centuries. Her recollections focused on the difficulties and hard work of dirt farming and on her girlhood and schooling in out-of-the-way rural areas and small towns.

These were to-the-West stories I heard in my childhood and adolescence from both sides of the family. The personal and highly individualized stories from my parents contained a special power. Theirs were usually stories of adventure, courage, and achievement, but also those of hardships and disappointments. The stories par-ticularly spoke to a son peering over the ridge of manhood, trying to understand what defined parents, place, and maturity. After two generations of my remem-bering, these narratives remain as early and lasting glimpses of a Father and Mother and a setting that still warm and shape a son's history and memories.

Millions of other Americans have listened to or read similar stories about fam-ilies, relatives, and friends who came west. In fact, stories of the frontier and American West still rival those of the American Civil War as the country's most popular tales. This brief book discusses a select number of these stories performed, lived out, or published in the century and more stretching from the end of the Civil War to the present. I use about twenty books, persons, movies, or other mediums to examine the ingredients of western stories, narratives that persisted relatively unchanged for a century but that have moved in notable new directions since the 1960s.

A few terms used in the following pages need elaboration. First of all, I utilize the words "western story" in a very general fashion. Although I have learned much about storytelling from such writers as William Cronon, Richard White, Robert Berkhofer, Hayden White, and Elliott West, this is a book about shifting interpretations of the American West rather than a theoretical study of storytelling. I do not mean to demean theoretical or cultural studies but merely to make clear that I have not followed those approaches. When I speak of "stories" or "narratives" (used interchangeably) about the West, I refer to the content more than to the structure of these interpretations. In the book's first two sections, I use the words "Wild West" to describe these stories because contemporaries invoked those terms. By the 1920s, "Western" had come into use for indicating stylized, formula fiction about the West. I employ this term in dealing with the popular fiction written about the West from Owen Wister to Louis L'Amour. Finally, I purposefully include a good deal of plot summary to clarify the continuing but also recently changing contents of western stories.

In the initial section of this study, Buffalo Bill Cody's Wild West show, the dime novel, and Frederick Jackson Turner's frontier thesis illustrate the Creation Stories formulated by 1900. Meanwhile, in the three generations stretching from the end of the Civil War to the mid-1920s, other western people and their experiences were omitted from the emerging western story. The second section utilizes the careers of two very different women, Mary Hallock Foote and Calamity Jane, the autobiography of Indian leader Geronimo, and the coauthored novel of Native American Mourning Dove to exemplify those whose lives and works represent Untold Stories.

At the opening of the twentieth century, most of the ingredients of what became the Western were in place. As the third section indicates, from the publication of *The Virginian* (1902) through the first of Louis L'Amour's immensely popular Westerns in the 1950s and 1960s, these Traditional Stories dominated fictional representations of the American West. Between the two world wars, widely circulating biographies of Old West characters, such as Walter Noble Burns's *Saga of Billy the Kid* (1926), prevailed among western biographies. During the same period, the classic film *Stagecoach* (1939) instanced the emergence and growing strength of Western movies by World War II. The final section discusses the dramatic changes that redefined the western story after the 1960s. Wallace Stegner's realistic regional novel *Angle of Repose* (1971), Patricia Nelson Limerick's New Western history *The Legacy of Conquest* (1987), Leslie Marmon Silko's ethnic novel *Ceremony* (1977), and Larry McMurtry's countermythic novel *Lonesome Dove* (1985) typify New Stories of the West surfacing in the last thirty years.

In brief compass, then, these lectures trace the evolution of the western story since the Civil War. Until the early 1960s, these stories followed familiar plot lines and character types. But shifting cultural attitudes, the influential fiction and films of several novelists and directors, and changing popular attitudes toward women, minority groups, and the environment in the decades since the 1960s helped transform the earlier stories, replacing them with new narratives. In stressing continuity more than change, these lectures provide a companion study to the author's recent book, *Re-imagining the Modern American West: A Century of Fiction, History, and Art* (1996). That study emphasized discontinuity over time through frontier, regional, and postregional re-imaginings of the West. Taking a different path, the present chapters treat a central story in American history, elucidating an archetypal American narrative that remains an important segment of American culture.

In the preparation of this volume, I have piled up several debts. First, my thanks go to my colleagues at the University of New Mexico Press and the UNM History Department for selecting me to give the annual Calvin Horn Lectures on Western History and Culture. The essence of this volume was presented in four lectures in Albuquerque, October 25–28, 1998. I am also indebted to the University of New Mexico for a Research Semester and a sabbatical leave during which most of this book was written. Deans William Gordon and Michael Fischer and History Chairs Jonathan Porter and Richard Robbins paved the way for these necessary leaves for research and writing. I also benefitted from two grants from the UNM Research Allocations Committee that facilitated my travel to pertinent libraries and archives.

I also wish to thank John Drayton of the University of Oklahoma Press, Charles Rankin of *Montana Magazine,* the editors of *Colorado Heritage,* Sam Scinta and Bob Baron of Fulcrum Publishing, and editors at Bedford Books for allowing me to use here material that first appeared in their publications. Along the way, Jen Clark, Angela Thomas, David Key, and Cindy Tyson helped me put the manuscript into final form. More recently David Key and Cindy Tyson read and helpfully commented on the entire manuscript. Professor James McLaird of Dakota Wesleyan University and William R. Whiteside of Cottage Hills, Illinois, read the section on Calamity Jane and saved me from factual and interpretive errors. Among my several colleagues in western history at the University of New Mexico, I wish to single out Paul Andrew Hutton, whose many informal discussions of the Old West and its interpreters have been a delight and continuous stimulation during the last decade and more. David Holtby at the University of New Mexico Press helped arrange the Calvin Horn Lectures and expeditiously shepherded the manuscript to publication. Finally, I owe many large and long-range debts to the persons named on the page of dedication.

Telling Western Stories

Prologue

Origins of the Western Story

EARLY IN JULY **1882,** more than one thousand horsemen from all over the central and northern plains came riding into North Platte, Nebraska. Answering Buffalo Bill Cody's invitation to a Fourth of July roundup, the riders invaded his hometown for an unforgettable exhibition of riding, roping, shooting, and "cowboy-fun."

The Old Glory Blow Out erupted from a string of unplanned events. Returning home after his hectic tenth year starring in dramas featuring Old West characters and frontier themes, Buffalo Bill discovered that North Platte had nothing on tap to celebrate Independence Day. When town fathers urged Cody to plan a July 4 roundup, he immediately set out to do so, mailing out five thousand handbills urging riders and other celebrants to join him for a memorable get-together of exhibitions and entertainment.[1]

The questions of organization and content that perplexed Cody in the early summer of 1882 have faced hundreds of other showmen, writers, and interpreters of the American West. How could he tell his story of the Wild West, what ingredients should his narrative contain, and how should he organize the segments of his story? For Cody, the answers came from his experiences as a frontiersman, especially his role as a famous scout, his years as an actor, and his emotional attachment to a disappearing frontier. He would cobble together the Old Glory Blow Out on a signal Fourth of July in North Platte from a Wild West he knew and loved.

Those noteworthy events in summer 1882 reveal much about Buffalo Bill's career as well as about the decades-long depiction of the frontier as the American Wild West since that time. The extraordinary success of the Old Glory Blow Out led Cody directly to his traveling Wild West, but it also helped him to formulate a popular frontier that dominated interpretations of the West well into the twentieth century. After more than a century of hindsight, it is clear that Buffalo Bill, more than any other figure, is responsible for what has become known as the myth of the American West.

Buffalo Bill Cody did not discover the Wild West, however. Instead, his story of the West built on several centuries of stories about the Wilderness Out There. From Ancient Times through the Middle Ages, Greeks, Romans, and Europeans often viewed the West as the direction to Elysium and Empire. In the sixteenth and seventeenth centuries, power-hungry leaders in Portugal, Spain, and England looked west for their future fiefdoms. Soon thereafter, when Spain, France, and England vied for dominion in the New World, the West remained for dreamers an oxymoronic combination of promised riches and threatening wilderness. Not surprisingly, the narratives of Spanish and English explorers and of the first settlers often praised the rich abundances of what they saw (or thought they saw) even while they warned new immigrants of the dangers awaiting them.[2]

These ambivalent reactions color many of the first literary and historical treatments of the American frontier. For example, Puritans urged coreligionists to undertake their "errand into the wilderness" and yet depicted that frontier as the domain of the Devil and his minions or, better yet, the Spanish and French. By the end of the eighteenth century, in frontier narratives only courageous military heroes or intrepid frontiersmen such as Daniel Boone seemed able to conquer the demanding wilderness. Other persons less able or ambitious, warned conservative New Englander Timothy Dwight and Virginian William Byrd, would be destroyed or lapse into boorish farmers and live like white trash or uncivilized Indians in a frontier "lubberland."[3]

During the first half of the nineteenth century, James Fenimore Cooper did more than any other writer to popularize the frontier. His widely read Leatherstocking Tales in the 1820s and 1830s provided American and European readers with a valiant hero who battled the wilderness and "barbaric" Indians to open the frontier for those coming behind. But at large costs, for Natty Bumppo was unable to remain in eastern society, never found a suitable mate, and was forced to live out his life isolated from family and hearth. So influential was Cooper's story line that it appeared repeatedly throughout the nineteenth century and profoundly influenced dime novelists and Local Color writers after the Civil War.

Before mid-century, explorers, historians, and artists added other ingredients to the story of the West. The Lewis and Clark, Stephen H. Long, and John C. Frémont accounts portrayed the trans-Mississippi West as a far-flung, gigantic series of landscapes, full of beauty, wonder, and dangers. Traveler Richard H. Dana and historian Francis Parkman furnished other portraits of life among the hide and tallow Californios and varied Indian groups of the Plains and Rockies. And the canvases of George Catlin, Karl Bodmer, and Alfred Jacob Miller startled viewers with their stunning portraits of Mandan and upper Missouri tribes and the intrepid mountain men who invaded and trapped those areas.[4]

By the outbreak of the Civil War, Americans had been treated to a variety of images and stories about the American frontier and West. After the hiatus of a fratricidal war and the following peace at Appomattox, new kinds of Wests appeared. For nearly a generation, journalists, government officials, and other travelers kept easterners well supplied with tales of frontier warfare with "savage" Indians. Even before those red-hot narratives began to lose popularity in the 1880s and 1890s, other stories of cattle trails and cowboys and outlaws and gunslingers captured thousands of readers. When eastern writer George Ward Nichols lionized James Butler ("Wild Bill") Hickok in *Harper's Magazine* as a frontier demigod armed with unerring pistols and limitless bravery, he helped launch a Wild West school of journalism that flourished for several generations.[5]

Nor should one underestimate the powerful impact of a clutch of sensational frontier incidents in the half-decade stretching from 1876 to 1881. From the dramatic demise of George Custer, the assassination of Wild Bill Hickok, and the historic appearance of Calamity Jane in Deadwood—all in the summer of 1876 as the nation celebrated its centennial—until the killing of Billy the Kid and the Shootout at the OK Corral in the summer and fall of 1881, the frontier was awash in startling stories of sensational conflicts. It was in these traumatic times of rumor and bold headlines that Buffalo Bill Cody launched his Wild West and helped formulate the western story.

Chapter One

Creation Stories

BUFFALO BILL'S WILD WEST did more than any other medium in the late nineteenth century to synthesize pre-existing ideas about the frontier and to present them in an entertaining, extraordinary way. By the end of the century, Americans had defined a mythic West, one crystallized and embodied in Cody's traveling arena show. More than contemporary dime novels, more than sensational newspaper stories, more than the siren calls of western tourist traps, and more than historian Frederick Jackson Turner's frontier thesis, Buffalo Bill's became *the* invented West Americans held in their mind's eye and in their hearts when they spoke of an Old West that seemed to be disappearing.

The largest question that faced Buffalo Bill loomed before all western storytellers in the late nineteenth century. How was one to tell these stories—or, better yet—how could one tell a story that interested audiences and made narrative sense of a remarkable frontier involving so many titanic characters? Undoubtedly, these questions were percolating in the fertile mind of William F. ("Buffalo Bill") Cody during the 1870s and early 1880s. As Buffalo Bill gradually discovered a way to tell his stirring story, he played a central role in inventing an American Wild West.

Buffalo Bill's youthful experiences, his years as a frontiersman and scout, and his ten years as an actor were important preparations for a later career as an intrepid showman celebrating a Wild West. Born in 1848, the son of an ambitious entrepreneurial father with itchy feet, Will Cody had already experienced several years of northern plains adventure before he became an orphan at seventeen. Hiring on as a wagon driver and trader while still in his teens, Cody crisscrossed much of the central interior West before serving briefly in the Civil War. He gained a reputation as a valiant and daring outrider, and local newspapers and government reports saluted his valuable work with the frontier army. Then a chance meeting in the summer of 1869 with author Edward Zane Carroll Judson (Ned Buntline) and the serialized publication of Buntline's sensational dime novel *Buffalo Bill, the King of the Border Men* in 1869–70 exploded Cody overnight into a nationally recognized hero.[1]

Buffalo Bill's rising star as a popular figure shone brightly in the next decade. In 1872, when the Grand Duke Alexis of Russia expressed a desire to hunt and experience the frontier firsthand, General Phil Sheridan, Cody's former commander, selected the "far-famed" scout to guide the expedition on a buffalo hunt. Dressing flamboyantly and playing the role of the skilled frontiersman for the international visitor, Buffalo Bill had, according to his biographer, "put on his first Wild West show, and he had made newspaper headlines."[2] Later that year when Cody went east, he was lionized as the living embodiment of the Wild West. By his mid-twenties, Buffalo Bill was becoming a living legend, hailed as the handsome, notorious scout of the prairies, already the hero of novels and a magic figure in western history. He was ready for something else.

That new opportunity came on stage. Appearing first as an actor in Chicago in December 1872, Cody became increasingly synonymous with an adventuresome frontier during the next few years. Buffalo Bill's initial appearance behind the footlights reveals much about the gargantuan appetites of audiences for western materials and illustrates as well the step-by-step formation of Cody as the quintessential showman and formulator of an invented Wild West. At first glance, one wonders how Buffalo Bill accomplished so much with such little talent and preparation. In Ned Buntline's drama *The Scouts of the Prairie,* reportedly written in four hours, Cody clearly proved his inadequacies as an actor. So did Texas Jack Omohundro. When Cody and Texas Jack forgot their lines, Buntline helped them to ad lib, filling in the earlier silences with scout talk and frontier yarns. And when ten out-of-work actors dressed as Indians were melodramatically dispatched, the audience cheered enthusiastically. The phony Indians were revived in the third act and once again wiped out. When the final curtain dropped, the packed makeshift theater thundered its approval.[3]

Despite these enthusiastic responses from audiences, newspaper critics often savaged Buffalo Bill's dramatic efforts in Chicago and in East Coast cities through June of 1873. Reviewing the initial performance, a reporter for the Chicago *Times* wrote: "Such a combination of incongruous drama, execrable acting, renowned performers, mixed audience, intolerable stench, scalping, blood and thunder, is not likely to be vouchsafed to a city a second time, even Chicago." A New York *World* reviewer also dismissed the play as "very poor slop." Although right about aesthetic points, these critics missed the larger attractiveness of Buffalo Bill's stage presentations. Audiences flocked to his plays not because of his acting skills but because he was, in person, an authentic frontiersman in an age that loved the frontier and tales about it. Early on, as Buffalo Bill's wife remembered, Cody admitted his limitations but also worked hard to improve. In St. Louis, after Cody recognized his wife in the audience, he stopped his Indian-killing long enough to come up stage to tell her: "Oh Mamma! . . . I'm a bad actor." And after the house roared its agreement, he added: "Honest, Mamma, . . . does this look as awful out there as it feels up here?"[4]

Here were early foreshadowings of Cody's developing genius as a showman. He became a master at working his audiences. An actor he was not, an able performer he quickly became. Capitalizing on his celebrity status as a famous frontier scout, Buffalo Bill increasingly took hold of his dramas, focused them on lively conflicts between scouts and Indians, and gave theater-goers what they seemed to want. Dropping Buntline as his manager, adding super publicist Major John Burke, and organizing the Buffalo Bill Combination (a drama troupe), Cody adeptly played on the insatiable interest in the Great West. Still, when he cajoled Wild Bill Hickok to participate in *Scouts of the Plains* in 1873–74, he got more than he hoped for. Although some considered Hickok, like Cody, a "living God behind the footlights," he refused to become an integral part of Cody's company. For Wild Bill, these performances were "foolish . . . play-acting"; he preferred to drink, flirt with the play's heroine, and powder burn the Indians (supposedly lying dead on stage) by firing his pistols close to their hairy legs. Abandoning the troupe because he considered their melodrama phony and untrue to the frontier he and Cody had known, Hickok retreated west.[5] Two and a half years later he lay dead in Deadwood, the victim of an assassin's bullet.

Cody's dramas played before packed houses at the same time that dramatic Wild West events captured newspaper headlines year after year. Continual conflicts with Indians, the Custer disaster at the Little Big Horn and Hickok's demise in 1876, the Lincoln County War in 1877–78, and the death of Billy the Kid and the Shootout at the OK Corral in 1881—these sensational episodes, as well as dozens of others, brought to a near fever pitch audience interest in a frenetic frontier.

Rosa Bonheur, *Col. W. F. Cody* (1889)

William F. ("Buffalo Bill") Cody did more than any other person to create the archetypal western story during the late nineteenth century. (Courtesy Buffalo Bill Historical Center, Cody, Wyoming)

Buffalo Bill epitomized the close correspondence between contemporary events in the West and staged history. Each summer Cody returned west, usually to take up his role as a much-recognized scout. One revealing moment in mid-summer 1876 merged the frontiersman and showman personas of Buffalo Bill. Like many others in the West, Cody was eager to take revenge for the annihilation of Custer and his men the previous June. When the Fifth Cavalry for which Buffalo Bill was scouting chanced upon a small group of Cheyenne Indians in the northwest corner of Nebraska on July 17, Cody, still dressed in his fancy acting regalia, shot and scalped the young chief Yellow Hand (actually Yellow Hair). As troopers rushed by Buffalo Bill to engage other Indians, he reportedly waved the war bonnet of his victim and shouted "First Scalp for Custer!" Within days, eastern newspapers trumpeted Cody's bravery, expanding the event into a hand-to-hand duel of legendary proportions.[6]

As often was the case, Cody easily participated in the puffery. In subsequent dramas, he agreed to act out an expanded version of the Yellow Hair story and proudly displayed the grisly trophy of the chief's scalp. Nor did he discourage his press agent John M. Burke from making the July 1876 incident into a epiphanic moment in the apotheosis of Buffalo Bill, the godlike hero of the Wild West. Further, Cody wrote or allowed his name to appear as author of several dime novels, he produced an autobiography with the indefatigable Burke, and he starred in new plays specifically written to feature his showmanship.[7]

But each year Buffalo Bill grew more tired of these footlight fantasies. Increasingly he chatted with Burke and others about a traveling, big-arena spectacle that, in Ned Buntline's words, would "take the prairies and the Injuns and everything else right to 'em" (the eastern public).[8] Several others were thinking along on similar lines. For example, Nat Salsbury, a man of evident managerial talents and experience, urged Cody to put together a spectacle of horsemanship and Indian fighting and to take it on the road. Financial pressures also played a determining role. Although Cody had taken in hundreds of thousands as an actor, he had little to show for his money. Perhaps the arena show would add markedly to his income even as it allowed him to present his idea of the Wild West. While he hesitated—and hoped—the clear success of the Old Glory Blow Out in July 1882 pushed him over the edge. Now he had to try something new.

Early in the fall of 1882 long-held dreams and recent successes finally drove Buffalo Bill to his first Wild West show. He was well aware, after the "sensational success" of the Old Glory Blow Out, that he had touched a vibrant cord of interest among Midwesterners.⁹ Now he had the opportunity to put together the outdoor spectacle celebrating the Old West that he had dreamed of for more than ten years. In the decade from 1883 to the momentous Columbian Exposition in 1893, Buffalo Bill Cody groped his way year by year toward the Wild West story he wanted to tell, thereby inventing the first internationally acclaimed story of the trans-Mississippi West.

What were the essential ingredients of Cody's story, and how did he organize those segments? In providing tentative answers to these significant questions, Buffalo Bill drew on his experiences as a frontiersman, as a dramatic showman, and with the recent Old Glory Blow Out. Obviously, the cowboys, especially the trick riders and ropers, had to play a central role. Buffalo Bill also wanted the Deadwood stage since it lent an authentic note, and he himself had ridden in it during the mid-1870s. Cody was convinced too that the Pony Express, particularly a dramatic scene of exchanging mail and horses, should be part of the extravaganza. Skilled marksmen like Capt. A. H. Bogardus, billed as "a champion clay-pigeon shot," must also be brought on board.

What to do about Native Americans was a more perplexing question. After casting about for possible Indian participants, especially Sioux, Cody accepted Gordon W. (Pawnee Bill) Lillie's offer to secure Oklahoma Pawnees for the troupe. In addition, Cody's neighbor and ranch partner, Major Frank North, agreed to participate as "The White Chief of the Pawnees."¹⁰ It must be remembered that since the Little Big Horn was but a half-dozen years in the past and since bands of Apache were still roaming free in the Southwest, many Americans and not a few showman were uneasy about having Indians as an integral part of an Old West celebration.

There were also the large problems of leadership. From his experience with the Buffalo Bill Combination, Cody knew that he worked best as a showman, not as a business partner, administrator, or publicist. Earlier, Cody and Nate Salsbury had chatted about a possible partnership to sponsor an outdoor pageant of the West, but when Cody decided to move ahead after mid-summer of 1882, Salsbury hesitated to consummate the partnership. He was more intrigued with a show celebrating horsemanship than the larger story Cody wanted to dramatize. With Salsbury unavailable, Cody turned to Dr. William F. Carver, a resident of Cody's hometown of North Platte, a participant in the Old Glory Blow Out, and self-advertised as the "Champion Shot of the World"

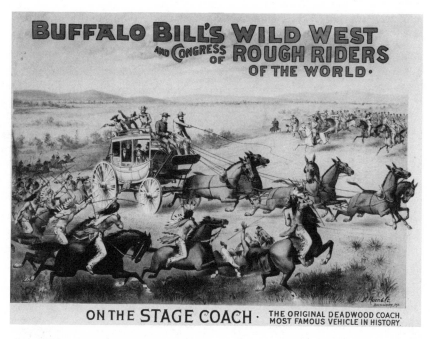

On the Stage Coach, circa 1887

Buffalo Bill's Wild West arena show, dramatizing dozens of memorable stories of competition, provided a pioneering cultural narrative for later western storytellers. (Courtesy Buffalo Bill Historical Center, Cody, Wyoming)

and the "Evil Spirit of the Plains." Once the temperamental Carver signed on, Salsbury refused to join Cody's efforts to organize the Wild West. The planning team was completed when Major John Burke, the evangelical wordsmith of Cody's limelight days, agreed to help plan the troupe's itinerary and to serve as the all-important propagandist for the Wild West.[11]

AFTER a hectic fall, winter, and spring of planning, scheduling, rehearsing, and fund-raising (Cody completed his final year of acting that fall and winter), the show opened at the Fair Grounds in Omaha on May 19. Billed as "The Wild West, Hon. W. F. Cody and Dr. W. F. Carver's Rocky Mountain and Prairie Exhibition," the celebration was an instant success. The next day an

Omaha headline gave the troupe a rousing assurance: "The 'Wild West' Sweeps All Victorious Before It. Eight Thousand People Attend the Initial Performances, And Go Wild With Enthusiasm—The Races, Fights And Feats of the Big Amusement Hit." After another performance in Omaha, the show headed east through Iowa and Illinois and then to New York and Boston during the summer, and back through Chicago to Omaha before disbanding in late fall.[12]

The sequence of scenes in the first Wild West show illustrates Buffalo Bill's early efforts to organize his narrative of the West. After an opening parade that featured all the gaudily dressed participants, the horses and wild animals, and a band, the nearly non-stop action began. A pony race among Indian riders led to the rapid exchange of horses and mail bags to illustrate the Pony Express. Then came the Indian attack on the Deadwood Stage, which was saved at the last moment by the heroic actions of Buffalo Bill and scouts (later cowboys). A race between an Indian on horseback and on foot came just before shooting feats by Capt. Bogardus, Doc Carver, and Buffalo Bill. Next, in one of the most popular features, cowboys took part in bronc riding, in lassoing steers, and in chasing a buffalo. A final scene, changed during the tour, featured an Indian dash or a conflict between Indians and scouts.[13]

Although Buffalo Bill told audiences and reporters he wanted "everything genuine" in his performance, he featured only action, adventure, and competition. If he took pains to avoid what he considered the side-show mentality of circuses, he nonetheless made sure that his avowed authenticity would not undercut his goal of entertaining every person who attended his show. Competition was the key word. From the races, through the shooting matches, to the attack on the stagecoach, and on to the "cowboy frolic," Cody loaded up his performance with lively competitions among his performers. By filling his Wild West show with appealing contests, Buffalo Bill defined the West as an arena for dramatic competitions with Native peoples and other opponents.[14]

Even before the 1883–84 season concluded, Cody was planning a better organized and more ambitious, eye-catching extravaganza. Finding the jealous and dyspeptic Doc Carver an impossible codirector, Buffalo Bill approached Nate Salsbury, who agreed to become a partner in the Wild West. The new match benefitted the entire troupe. An experienced manager and traveler, Salsbury provided important balance to Cody's mounting reputation as a showman and performer but also his distinct limitations as an organizer. Later, Salsbury grew to resent Buffalo Bill's deification, even while his administrative acumen helped keep the troupe fiscally sound and on schedule. Until his death in 1902, Salsbury did more than any other person, except Cody, to put the Wild West year after year before millions of viewers.[15]

New acts were also added. Realizing the need for a more dramatic closing scene, Cody organized "The Attack on the Settler's Cabin," which, according to a Boston newspaper, was "intensely dramatic and exciting, and conveyed a vivid and realistic idea of the perils of border life."[16] In 1885, another sensational episode, Cody's battle with Yellow Hand, the "First Scalp for Custer," added another theatrical vista. One year later, Buck Taylor played the role of Custer in a new segment depicting the Battle of the Little Big Horn. Eventually known as the "King of the Cowboys," the 6' 4" Taylor also greatly enlivened the "Cowboy Frolic" section of the show with his acrobatic riding and roping antics. Even more attention-catching was the notorious Sitting Bull, who joined the Wild West for the summer of 1885. Given top billing in the show's publicity, and paid fifty dollars a week for his participation, the Hunkpapa Sioux chief rode in the processional with Buffalo Bill but did not take part in the competitions.[17]

Although it may not have seemed so at the time, the most important addition to the troupe came when Annie Oakley joined the show during the 1885 season. A shy farm girl from Ohio, Annie Moses Butler (known professionally as Annie Oakley) had already built a reputation for superb marksmanship in variety shows and with traveling shows. Since Cody had several shooting stars, he was reluctant to hire another. But Annie's trick shooting attracted immediate attention, so she and her manager-husband Frank Butler were hired. For seventeen years, "Little Missie," as Cody called her, remained with the Wild West as its most popular star, next to Buffalo Bill. In addition to being a superb shot and a dependable, no-nonsense performer, Annie served as an attraction for women, particularly those who wondered about all the shooting and frenetic action in Cody's show. Through most of her years with the Wild West, Annie opened the show with her dramatic shooting skills.[18]

Despite continuing difficulties with travel and scheduling and all the frictions involved with a troupe numbering two hundred to three hundred persons, the seasons of 1884, 1885, and 1886 were increasingly successful. Hundreds of thousands of spectators came to see and thrill to Cody's blend of action, competition, and conflict. Sometimes single shows drew 40,000 and during one week in New York City in July 1886, attendance boomed to nearly 200,000.[19] Then came the invitation that changed everything. Would the Wild West come to London to participate in the American Exhibition as part of

Queen Victoria's Golden Jubilee celebrating her half-century as England's queen. Salsbury and Cody quickly accepted the invitation.

The familiar ingredients of the Wild West remained much the same during the troupe's stay in England from April 1887 until May 1888. But the circumstances surrounding the first of the show's several international trips transformed its impact. The perspicacious Salsbury, understanding the necessity of balancing tradition and novelty, predicted success in England. He told an American reporter "Over there [England] the curiosity to see redmen, cowboys, and all the other features of this exhibition is greater even than here."[20] For English people of all kinds, from Queen Victoria, who found time during the Jubilee celebrations to visit the show, to the hundreds of thousands from London and outlying areas, the Wild West was a magnificent, riveting demonstration of what they already believed about the history and character types of a faraway, magic frontier.

Salsbury's prediction of success proved remarkably prescient. The English, the queen included, relished the opportunity to meet Annie Oakley, Buck Taylor, the Indians and their families, and other personalities. They saw Buffalo Bill and his entourage as living embodiments of the fictional frontier heroes of James Fenimore Cooper and Bret Harte and the dime novels, all of which circulated widely in England. The cowboys and "Red Indians," particularly, intrigued audiences as representations of an American Wild West. One British actor summed up this fascination: "'the great mass of the English people think of America as a place principally infested by Indians, bears, and hunters, and they took Bill and his show as a sample.'"[21] In fact, so imprinting were these impressions that well into the twentieth century the English thought of Buffalo Bill's exhibition as a genuine depiction of the American frontier and West.

After spending much of the period from 1888 to 1892 in Europe, the Wild West returned home. Fresh from international triumphs that took it to several major European cities, Cody's exhibition may have reached an even higher plane of popularity and significance as part of the Columbian Exposition in Chicago. The 1893 season was, writes the leading authority on the Wild West, "to be his [Buffalo Bill's] biggest and best—some have said the most prosperous in outdoor show business."[22] Ironically, when Cody and Salsbury's request to be physically a part of the Chicago World's Fair grounds was denied, they rented for $180,000 an expansive fourteen-acre area directly across from the fair's main entrance. Anyone who visited the huge fairgrounds passed by the gate to the Wild West. Decorating the Wild West grounds like a modern-day Frontierland and playing on historical continuities, the planners of the show advertised Christopher Columbus as "Pilot of the Ocean, the First Pioneer" and Buffalo Bill as "Pilot of the Prairie, the Last Pioneer" and displayed the frontier cabins of Teddy Roosevelt and the recently assassinated Sitting Bull. From the opening performance on April 26 to its close on November 1, the show was a smashing financial success. Newspapers, local businessmen, and national public figures saluted Cody's exhibition, praising its authenticity and its moral content and family entertainment.[23]

Now billed as "Buffalo Bill's Wild West and Congress of Rough Riders of the World," the exhibition had been expanded to nineteen events, including the initial Grand Review and the final Salute. Familiar events included Annie Oakley, Johnny Baker, and Buffalo Bill as featured sharpshooters, horse and foot races among Indians and international riders and runners, the antics of cowboys, the Pony Express exhibit, and attacks on the Deadwood Stage and the Settler's Cabin. Revealing the influences of the troupe's recent stay in Europe were the "Congress of Rough Riders," horsemen and military riders from throughout the world. Other newer events were the Emigrant Train, which included an Indian attack on covered wagons and the timely rescue by Buffalo Bill and his scouts and cowboys. Cody also expanded the sections on Indians and added another lively scene called the Buffalo Hunt. In August, he changed the final spectacle to a dramatic rendition of the Battle of the Little Big Horn, or Custer's Last Charge. Reporters and audiences alike agreed that this stirring scene brought increased drama and pathos to the show's story.[24]

By all accounts the Wild West show of 1893 was an astounding success. At season's end, Cody and associates, despite all the added costs of a new setting and expanded scenes, had cleared more than one million dollars. All the scheduled performances, sometimes involving more than four hundred participants, came off as promised, rain or shine. Nearly twenty-five thousand persons daily flocked to the show, meaning that about five million people saw the show. Put another way, about one of five visitors to the Chicago World's Fair also experienced the Wild West. Glowing newspaper accounts seemed little more than publicity releases for the show. The Chicago *Daily News* gushed that "No other exhibition . . . has received the plaudits of the people as has Buffalo Bill's Wild West." Crack reporter Amy Leslie of the same newspaper opined that "No such an engaging story-teller as Buffalo Bill figures in history or romance. He is quiet, rich in humor and mellow in his style as a bottle of old port." Turning interpreter, she added: "He sticks to truth mainly and is more intensely beguiling than the veriest maker of fiction."[25]

In his mid-forties, after eleven years on the road with the Wild West, Buffalo Bill was at the height of his showman powers. He had an international reputation, and some thought of him as the best-known figure in the United States. For two more decades Cody kept at his work even though often threatening to retire to his ranch and family. In those post-1893 years he worked current events into the show, including the Spanish American War and World War I. The core of what he wanted to say about the West was already clear, however. Those familiar emphases continued to the end of his days.[26]

That thematic core, according to well-known western historian Richard White, was violence, as distinct from the agricultural, nonviolent frontier of contemporary historian Frederick Jackson Turner.[27] Violence was the key ingredient of the attacks on the Settler's Cabin, the Emigrant Train, the Deadwood Stage, and in Custer's Last Stand, but these four scenes (and they rarely if ever all appeared in one show) were but three or four of fifteen to twenty scenes. Rather than violence, *competition* was Cody's main focus. The horse and foot races, the sharpshooter contests, and the roping and trick riding featured competition. Like a series of interlocking tableaus, these interest-whetting scenes functioned as a whole, emphasizing Buffalo Bill's conviction that the Wild West adventure tested the courage and daring of participants through demanding competitions. From the opening to the final scenes, the annual Wild West shows emphasized contests. In following his own experiences and perceptions, Cody invented a Wild West story that depicted the frontier as an arena for contestatory actions. As Buffalo Bill and his troupe told this story year after year for several decades, the narrative so fastened itself to the consciousness of audiences that his Wild West became theirs. In his penchant of pageantry, Cody formulated a mythic story of adventure, drama, and competition that a century later remains a notable Creation Story of American history.

IF BUFFALO BILL and his Wild West show were the most powerful shaping force in molding images of an American Wild West between the Civil War and 1900, several other actors played important supporting roles in this myth-producing drama. The most conspicuous of these other actors were the dime novelists. From 1860 to the turn of the century the American reading public was awash in dime novels. Several publishers and hundreds of writers turned out dime and nickel novels by the railroad car load. Although dime novelists utilized a plethora of topics and heroes, fiction set on the frontier or in the trans-Mississippi West topped the popularity polls. In fact, a survey of fifteen hundred novels issued by the Beadle and Adams, the most prolific of the early publishers, revealed that approximately 75 percent dealt with frontier subjects, with a majority of these depicting the West beyond the Mississippi. So popular were western dime novels that several other companies, capitalizing on that interest, launched their own dime novel series.[28]

Two dime novels published in 1860, the first year such works appeared, illustrate the themes and emphases dime novelists abandoned and those they increasingly adopted in the next two generations. In the 1860s and 1870s, the dime novel clearly shifted from the ethnic feminine focus in Ann S. Stephens's *Malaeska: The Indian Wife of the White Man,* including its depiction of a gray and tragic frontier, to a white, masculine, heroic, and triumphalist frontier in Edward S. Ellis's *Seth Jones; or, The Captives of the Frontier.* Ellis's dime novel sold more than 500,000 copies and quickly became the most powerful model for hundreds of others. In following many of the plots, character types, class roles, and settings that James Fenimore Cooper employed, and in "appropriating the wilderness for the glorification of white men rescuing white women and killing Native Americans," argues critic Christine Bold, "this version of the frontier adventure . . . held sway thereafter in the Beadle production line and its imitators."[29]

Using hunters, scouts, frontier detectives, and then cowboys around which to structure their sensational stories, dime novelists abandoned Cooper's excessive emphasis on class differences to suggest that courage, fortitude, and strength, more than pedigree and heritage, motivated westerners. In stressing that successes followed more from courageous competitions than from class backgrounds, the stories of western dime novels echoed the democratic, individualistic themes of Buffalo Bill and his traveling Wild West.[30]

Yet continuities as well as changes marked the half-century dividing Cooper and the dime novelists. Linking Daniel Boone and Cooper's Natty Bumppo to the later dime novelists, in a straight line of influence, was the need to portray frontier heroes as civilization bringers. As in George Caleb Bingham's wonderfully evocative painting *Daniel Boone Escorting Settlers through the Cumberland Gap* (1851–52), Boone and similar frontier figures are depicted as invading the wilderness to push back "savagery." Of course, if negative, destructive impulses took hold, these men became vicious Indian haters, driven by a violent brutishness and lapsing into the uncivilized "savagery" they attacked. But the Boone-Natty hero avoided such excesses, thus preparing the way for families and settled society that followed. Heroes of this stripe can be traced directly from the early nineteenth century into dime novels of the 1870s and 1880s.

Over time, the dime novelists realized that their readers wanted heroes who exhibited both eastern genteel and western democratic trappings. As Daryl Jones, the leading authority on the dime novel Western points out, a "hybrid hero" gradually developed, one who symbolized

> the wilderness skills and unlimited freedom of the Western hero, and the youth, gentility, and romantic potential of the eastern hero. Not until the creation of fictional characters modeled after Kit Carson or Buffalo Bill . . . [did] a hero of these unique proportions[31]

appear. Or, to invoke another rich cultural figure of the early nineteenth century, the dime novelists were creating fictional Andrew Jackson characters, fusions of courage, tenacity, and inner resources but also ones free from frontier boorishness and social inadequacies. Characters such as these were saved from earlier provincial dialects and backwoods humor and clothed in respectable English and acceptable deportment, making them acceptable mates for romantic heroines.

The hundreds of dime novels produced about Buffalo Bill reveal how jumbled were frontier fact and fiction and how often Cody's Wild West and the dime novel combined to produce the most popular images of the West from the late 1860s to 1900. More than 550 Buffalo Bill dime novels were published in the United States, with about a fifth of them written by Prentiss Ingraham. But Ned Buntline authored the first, and perhaps the most influential dime novel about Cody, *Buffalo Bill, the King of Border Men,* serialized in twelve installments from December 23, 1869, to March 10, 1870, in Street and Smith's *New York Weekly.* Buntline had talked and scouted with Cody a few days in the fall of 1869, hurried back to the East, and wrote his breathless fiction. Termed by its publishers "The Greatest Romance of the Age," Buntline's *Buffalo Bill* was an immediate bestseller.[32] Some think it did more than anything else to invent the legendary Buffalo Bill.

Ned Buntline, *Buffalo Bill, the King of the Border Men* (1869–70)

Ned Buntline's dime novel about Buffalo Bill, *Buffalo Bill, the King of the Border Men*, was a powerful shaping force in establishing the scout as an important western hero. The first installment appeared in Street & Smith's *New York Weekly*, December 23, 1869.

Buntline clearly imagined a great deal. He pictures Cody as something of a younger Cooper Leatherstocking hero. Buntline's Buffalo Bill sports a full beard, carries a rifle, and rides a horse. Here, Buffalo Bill, a skilled frontiersman and Indian fighter, speaks without dialect and exhibits extraordinary humility along with his bravery and courage. Much of the time he is protecting the virtue of his twin sisters or accompanying Wild Bill Hitchcock [*sic*] on a series of wild escapades. Unlike most other dime novelists, Buntline provides Buffalo Bill with a love interest, Louisa or Louise La Valliere, whom he rescues and later marries. She faintly resembles Louisa Frederici, who became Cody's wife in March 1866.

Buntline's astonishingly successful novel, puffed glowingly by his publisher, then became the basis for a very popular play *Buffalo Bill, the King of the Bordermen*. The dime novel, the play, and editor James Gordon Bennett's descriptions of Buffalo Bill as "the beau ideal of the plains" in the *New York Herald* made him a celebrated westerner on the East Coast.[33] Soon thereafter, as we have seen, Buntline talked Cody into starring in his own plays, and the theatrical Cody appeared alongside the frontier Buffalo Bill.

Throughout the 1870s—and for the next generation—Buffalo Bill dime novels appeared annually by the dozens. Cody even wrote a few of the novels himself, but the major producer of the Buffalo Bill dime novels was Prentiss Ingraham. The son of a minister and a soldier for the Confederacy, Ingraham was, he claimed, as swashbuckling as the pirates and filibusters about which he wrote. Early in the 1870s he already was churning out two dime novels a month, and it's estimated he wrote more than a thousand tales before his death in 1904.

Probably Ingraham produced his first work about Buffalo Bill in 1876, a story entitled *The Crimson Trail; or On Custer's Last Warpath*. In the next twenty-five years Ingraham churned out dozens and dozens of dime novels and other stories about Buffalo Bill. He may even have ghost-written some of Cody's autobiographical accounts; he certainly rivaled John M. Burke as the chief press agent for deifying Buffalo Bill. Once the Wild West show was launched in 1883, Ingraham sometimes traveled with the extravaganza, wrote publicity for the show, and produced, annually, an average of nearly ten dime novels a year, with an astounding twenty-three about Buffalo Bill in 1896.[34]

Although generalizing about Ingraham's more than one hundred works treating Buffalo Bill is tricky, a few observations are useful. Splendidly dressed, heroic, a gambler, Ingraham's protagonist is a chivalrous man who is gentle and gracious with maidens. But he can be violent too, especially in decimating Indians and in dispatching evil rascals who seem to appear just often enough to test Buffalo Bill's prowess. Even more significant as a forewarning of cowboy fictional heroes of the early twentieth century, Ingraham's valiant men often step outside the law to uphold justice that ineffectual society fails to uphold. Their actions can outweigh courtroom decisions because they're motivated by a clear, unassailable sense of justice. In this way, Ingraham's Buffalo Bill obviously adumbrates the vigilante actions of Owen Wister's Virginian.

In one of his earliest and best-known dime novels, *Adventures of Buffalo Bill, from Boyhood to Manhood* (1881), a semi-biographical work, Ingraham provides a central symbol for understanding the cultural significance of Buffalo Bill. In an opening description, he places Cody at the center of the western story emerging in the late nineteenth century. Buffalo Bill, Ingraham writes,

> will go down to history as one of America's strange heroes who has loved the trackless wilds, rolling plains and mountain solitudes of our land, far more than the bustle and turmoil, the busy life and joys of our cities, and who has stood as a barrier between civilization and savagery, risking his own life to save the lives of others.[35]

If the popular images of Buffalo Bill provide one notable link between Cooper's hero Natty Bumppo and protagonists of popular Westerns in the early twentieth century, the character of Deadwood Dick in a series of dime novels in the 1870s and 1880s furnished another important ingredient in the development of the western hero. Like the protagonists in many other road agent or outlaw dime novels, Deadwood Dick is forced outside the law to gain revenge on malefactors because the law, the courts, and society itself fail to indict the evildoers. In the decade following the first appearance of Deadwood Dick in 1877, his creator Edward L. Wheeler produced nearly thirty other dime novels about his hero and his exploits throughout the Far West.[36]

From his first appearance in Wheeler's *Deadwood Dick, the Prince of the Road; or, The Black Rider of the Black Hills* (1877), the outlaw hero represents the worker who has fled west to gain freedom from crooked eastern capitalists. Disguised as a road agent, Deadwood Dick attempts to gain revenge on his chief persecutors, Alexander and Clarence Filmore, who have robbed him and his sister, chased Dick from his adoptive home, and abused him. In turn, Dick has purloined money rightfully his and now, once in the West, he calls for the hanging of these murderous brothers because an uncaring society fails to pass and uphold laws protecting good people from such evil men. At the end of the novel Dick discloses his real name is Edward Harris and cries out "Now, I am inclined to be merciful to only those who have been merciful to me. . . . Boys, *string 'em up!*"[37]

The outlaw hero's essential goodness and his role as an upholder of justice are also at the center of Wheeler's best-known dime novel *Deadwood Dick on Deck; or, Calamity Jane, the Heroine of Whoop-Up* (1878). Here too the hero, guilty of illegal actions, has bruised the law in becoming an advocate for, a champion of, those under the lion's paw of corrupt officials and elite classes. Road agent figures like Deadwood Dick were immensely popular in pulp literature from the 1870s through the 1890s because they served as Robin Hoods rearranging inequitable class lines and power based on privileged birth, elite families, and ill-gotten wealth. In spite of their unlawful actions, Deadwood Dick and his sidekicks, roaming the trans-Mississippi West, are treated as good men, gentle to women, kindly to the helpless, and (underneath their masks or disguises) handsome individuals of magnetic grace and polish.

By the late 1870s and early 1880s another hero who became a major figure in early twentieth-century Westerns, the cowboy, began to appear as a supporting character in several dime novels. Because "cow-boys," as they were then called, had gained undeserved reputations as ne'er-do-well wanderers and sometimes as antisocial misfits of violent temperaments, dime novelists were hard put to turn them immediately into positive protagonists. Still, their lives as horsemen on the vast, open western plains were inviting material for romantic yarns for popular novelists searching for new material.[38]

Not surprisingly, dime novelists emphasized the externals of cowboy life. The dress, the horse riding, and the ranch settings are major ingredients of cowboy dime novels, rather than the specifics of branding, dehorning, and cutting. Even more important, as one authority notes, "dime novelists characterized the cowboy in the same fashion as they had characterized earlier Western heroes: they continued to externalize the Western hero's natural nobility, and they continued to stress his ambivalent relationship to established social and legal codes."[39] With a longer line of continuity in mind, one might observe that similar cowboy heroes become major figures in the fictional Westerns of Owen Wister and Zane Grey and the cinematic Westerns of William S. Hart and Tom Mix in the first decades of the twentieth century.

Several dime novels by Frederick Whittaker, Prentiss Ingraham, and William Patten, among hundreds of others, employ cowboy figures as generic dime

Edward L. Wheeler, *Deadwood Dick on Deck* (1878)

The Deadwood Dick dime novel series by Edward L. Wheeler featured the hero as a good/badman who frequently resorted to illegal actions to bring justice to the frontier. Calamity Jane was often his companion, sometimes his wife.

novel heroes. Although Whittaker is less inclined than other dime novelists to turn the cowboy into a demigod in leather pants, he celebrates their courage and natural abilities in *Parson Jim, King of the Cowboys* (1882). In this and other novels, he depicts cowboys as galloping into town "crazy with excitement and drink," as "lawless and uncultured" primitives.[40]

The most influential dime novel about cowboys, however, was Prentiss Ingraham's *Buck Taylor, King of the Cowboys,* which appeared in Beadle's Half-Dime Library in 1887. Like so many dime novels masquerading as biographies, Ingraham's work lauds the person and deeds of Buck Taylor, the star cowboy in Buffalo Bill's Wild West. In a fantastic, perpetual-action plot, Buck kills two Indians, outwits a whole band of renegades, fights an outfit of Mexicans, and escapes after being buried alive. Sensationalizing the King of the Cowboys much as he had Buffalo Bill a decade earlier, Ingraham lionizes Taylor in a 1891 novel as "the very *beau ideal* of a Texas cowboy . . . [whose] face was one to remember when once seen, beardless, youthful, yet full of character and fearlessness, amounting to reckless daring."[41] In another work issued the same year, Buck and his fellow riders are saluted as reminders of nature's noblemen:

> A reckless lot of men they were, light-hearted, entirely fearless, generous, noble in the treatment of a friend or fallen foe, and though feared by evil-doers and red-skins, they were admired and respected by the soldiers and the people of the settlements.[42]

At much the same time William G. Patten also glorified the cowboys as good men and true. Especially known as the originator of the popular hero Dick Merriwell, Patten depicts a typical cowboy in his dime novel *Wild Vulcan the Lone Rider* as "one of those grand creations of the mountains and plains, a young nobleman of nature." Later, in a series of novels about Cowboy Chris written under the pen name of William West Wilder, Patten depicts his young rider as a man who easily dispatches Apaches, who thinks it his "duty to aid the weaker party," and who is a "perfect *man,* being one of those persons women regard with frank admiration."[43]

By the mid-1890s, at the same time that Buffalo Bill's depiction of the frontier in his Wild West show had worked its way into the minds and hearts of millions of Americans, dime novelists had created and deified a series of attractive protagonists in their widely circulated stories. Even more noteworthy, they provided in the cowboy a new sun god who, within the next decade, became the darling of a fresh crop of novelists, of artists like Frederic Remington and Charles Russell, and of the newest of all mediums, the movies.

In still another important way, the dime novelists added what many readers considered authentic elements to the western story. Because these novelists were often like roving journalists looking for fresh stories and sensational characters, they frequently produced novels about Wild West characters before biographers caught up with those figures. For example, Buffalo Bill, Wild Bill Hickok, Calamity Jane, Belle Starr, and Billy the Kid first appeared in dime novels or romantic, and sometimes lurid, newspaper or magazine stories before they were the subjects of well-researched biographies.[44] This lag meant that millions of readers, having devoured the quickly issued dime novels or journalistic accounts, already had strongly in mind a series of sensational stories about the leading Wild West characters and episodes by the mid-1890s, well before sound biographies and histories appeared. The fund of exaggerated stories and rumors markedly shaped the novels, films, and popular accounts of the Wild West issued in the next two generations.

Although Buffalo Bill Cody and the dime novelists were the most influential popularizers of the Wild West story during the late nineteenth century, they were not the only shapers of this narrative. For example, their cousins in the popular story weeklies often produced serials remarkably similar in form and content to the dime novel Westerns. Writers like Ned Buntline and Prentiss Ingraham were also well-known contributors to the story weeklies. Nor should one overlook the shaping influences of journalists, especially those sent west to report on military-Indian conflicts, Wild West heroes and heroines, and controversial events like the Battle at the Little Big Horn, the Lincoln County War, or the Johnson County War. The on-the-spot stories that reporters filed often gave eastern readers tidbits about a Wild West they yearned to learn about and perhaps to visit. Like the dime novelists, journalists usually emphasized the lively aspects of their reports, thereby "wilding up" the West.[45]

These strains of the western story seemed to converge in the early 1890s. In addition to Buffalo Bill's extremely popular Wild West show, the ubiquitous dime novel, and thousands of newspaper and magazine stories, artists like Frederic Remington and authors such as Theodore Roosevelt and Emerson Hough dealt with the historical cowboy, and fictionists Alfred Henry Lewis and Owen Wister invoked the hired man on horseback for their short stories and novels in the first half of the 1890s.

IN THE SAME watershed years of the 1890s, professional historians, most notably the young Frederick Jackson Turner, discovered a closed frontier and an emerging Wild West. Most often, Turner is cited as the patriarch of the frontier school, by turns lionized and then criticized for arguing that the frontier was the most significant force in shaping an exceptional American character. A product of small-town Wisconsin, an enthusiastic outdoorsman, and a young man addicted to history and rhetoric, Turner early on fell in love with the frontier past and maintained the sustaining love affair until his death in the early 1930s. Completing bachelor's and master's degrees at the University of Wisconsin and a Ph.D. at the Johns Hopkins University, Turner returned to the Madison campus to spread the frontier doctrine in the 1890s.[46]

In a series of provocative essays between 1890 and 1893, Turner launched a western story of central importance to American historical writing well into the twentieth century. Simply put, he told his colleagues and students they were looking in all the wrong places to understand American exceptionalism. Like a good drill leader, Turner ordered his troops to do an about face. They must stop looking for American identity in European history and institutions; they must examine, instead, the American frontier experience as it advanced from the Atlantic to the Pacific. As he wrote in 1892, "American history up to our own day has been colonial history, the colonization of the Great West. This ever retreating frontier of free land is the key to American development." Turner ended this essay entitled "Problems in American History" with one of his characteristic rhetorical flourishes: "What the Mediterranean Sea was to the Greeks, breaking the bond of custom, offering new experiences, calling out new institutions and activities, that ever retreating Great West has been to eastern United States directly, and to the nations of Europe more remotely."[47]

The next year Turner delivered the most important position paper ever presented by an American historian. Revealingly, in his classic essay on "The Significance of the Frontier in American History," read before the American Historical Association meeting in Chicago in 1893 and less than five miles from Buffalo Bill's Wild West extravaganza, Turner clarified what kind of western story historians ought to tell. First, they should focus on the frontier. In one terse sentence, he encapsulated his major themes about the frontier: "The existence of an area of free land, its continuous recession, and the advance of American settlement westward, explain American development." His colleagues must tell this story, he added, because the frontier had contributed so many "traits" to the American experience. A "composite nationality," the

Frederick Jackson Turner

In 1893, the historian Frederick Jackson Turner spoke before a group of historians about "The Significance of the Frontier in American History." He urged researchers and readers to be more analytical in the stories they told about the American frontier and West. (Courtesy the University Archives, University of Wisconsin, Madison, Wisconsin)

"growth of democracy," independent individualism, and economic and physical mobility—all these characteristics and more could be traced to the frontier.[48] Any historical storyteller worthy of attention must understand how the frontier had placed its marks so widely and deeply on American history.

Less well known but equally important were Turner's attempts to reorient contemporary interpretations of the frontier West. As he told a correspondent nearly three decades later, other writers in the 1880s and early 1890s had been too caught up in depicting the frontier as a Wild West. Rather than analyzing the significance of notable frontier institutions, they had chronicled the lively events or heroic demigods of a frenetic frontier. As he had in his efforts to turn historians away from an excessive emphasis on American slavery and European traditions, Turner endeavored to lead interpreters of the West toward more analytical and less romantic views of their subject.[49]

From the opening pages of his seminal essay of 1893, Turner separated himself from writers who stressed the confrontational and exciting themes of Wild West history. Instead, he was intrigued with the continuing evolution, over time, of political, constitutional, and social institutions of a westward-moving frontier. Rather than limit his focus to a dramatic, sometimes violent meeting of opponents in the wilderness, the Wisconsin historian wanted to tell a frontier story that featured the evolutionary character of institution building. If this reorientation in frontier historical writing did not occur, Turner implied, popularizers would continue to invent and sell a fantastic, sensationalized, and phony Old West.

In still other ways, Turner put clear, explicit distance between himself and romanticists in his 1893 essay. Unfortunately, these differences seem unclear to recent revisionists who link Turner with Wild West aficionados. Turner made the distinctions explicit, however, when he wrote "much has been written about the frontier from the point of view of border warfare and the chase, but as a field for the serious study of the economist and the historian it has been neglected." For Turner, earlier historians like Francis Parkman and later writers like his contemporaries Theodore Roosevelt, Justin Winsor, or Rueben Gold Thwaites too often stressed an adventurous frontier, or they failed to adopt an interpretive approach to the frontier past. Turner tried to warn his listeners and readers away from these misguided notions about the western past.[50]

Turner saved his sharpest darts for those he considered the greater sinners. A key but often overlooked footnote in the frontier essay illuminates Turner's disgust with thrilling accounts of a Wild West. "I have refrained from dwelling on the lawless characteristics of the frontier," he writes, "because they are sufficiently well known. The gambler and desperado, the regulators of the Carolinas and the vigilantes of California, are types of that line of scum that the waves of advancing civilization bore before them, and of the growth of spontaneous organs of authority where legal authority was absent."[51] Who wrote about and dramatized this "line of scum" that Turner so detested? Perhaps reluctant to name names, Turner probably referred to Local Color writers and dime novelists who wilded up a West stretched well beyond the facts. The western Local Color stories of Bret Harte, Alfred Henry Lewis, and Joaquin Miller, widely read fictionists and poet, had celebrated gamblers, desperadoes, prostitutes, and romantic explorers and cowboys since the 1860s. Even in more lurid fashion, other eastern writers turned out thousands of dime novels dramatizing a West of scouts, "savages," renegades, and lively cowboys. By 1890, fiction and a good deal of historical writing about the West treated readers to a steady diet of incredulous adventure stories, far divorced from the historical reality Frederick Jackson Turner sought.

Most of all, Turner attempted to counter the large influence of Buffalo Bill's Wild West. Contrary to Turner's call for analytical, interpretive history of the frontier, Buffalo Bill carefully blended competition, conflict, and violence in his stirring narrative of a romantic West. Revealingly, the same day Turner delivered his frontier thesis at the Chicago World's Fair in July 1893, about five miles away Buffalo Bill paraded his frontier retinue before an audience of several thousand enthusiastic spectators. Avoiding Cody's Wild West show, Turner also contradicted Buffalo Bill's and similar interpretations of the frontier that emphasized melodramatic and sensational stories.[52] Even though recent interpreters sometimes link Turner and late nineteenth-century depictions of a Wild West, throughout Turner's early career he roundly criticized exaggerated accounts of an untamed Wild West, calling instead for careful studies of the frontier's significance. Just as Turner challenged earlier slavery-driven and European germ theory interpretations of American history, he sidelined Wild West versions to clear the way for his more explanatory approach.

Two traditions for interpreting the frontier and American West, then, were emerging in the 1890s. One, much influenced by the Cooper, Buffalo Bill, and dime novel tradition, pictured the West as a wild, untrammeled place, hosting free, adventuresome, and courageous men competing with Natives and awesome landscapes. The other tradition, much tied to Frederick Jackson Turner and academics who accepted the Turner or frontier interpretation, examined and sometimes celebrated that frontier experience as the most significant ingredient of American history and culture. Ironically, as revisionists criticize or even skewer Turner, they more often are lambasting the Wild West tradition, which Turner himself harpooned. A second irony becomes clear when one realizes that Turner's emphasis on the frontier helped keep alive the more popular Wild West tradition. In analyzing what he considered the democratic, individualistic, and "free land" influences and opportunities of migrating frontiers, Turner aided and abetted, unconsciously, aficionados who loved, championed, and staged a Wild West for similar reasons but for different purposes.

By the late 1890s, then, the scene was set for the appearance of the fully costumed western story. Within two generations, the fictional Western solidified into a recognizable pattern, from Owen Wister through Zane Grey and Ernest Haycox. The full flowering of this tradition came in the amazingly popular Westerns of the prolific Louis L'Amour. Romantic biographies by several writers, but particularly Walter Noble Burns's lively lifestory of Billy the Kid, also demonstrated how much these authors followed in and added to the western story. Meanwhile, silent films starring the likes of Broncho Billy Anderson, William S. Hart, and Tom Mix prepared the way for Western epics of the 1920s and the classic Western film *Stagecoach,* directed by John Ford and featuring John Wayne.

Before the florescence of the western story can be traced in the first half of the twentieth century, however, one must recognize and understand the voices left out of these Creation Stories. As we shall see in the next chapter, the lives of women and the experiences of Native Americans often remained Untold Stories.

Chapter Two

Untold Stories

AT THE OPENING of the twentieth century, the ingredients necessary for a classic story of the Wild West were available to a talented and insightful writer able to understand and synthesize these materials. That writer and book had not yet appeared, but they soon would in Owen Wister's runaway best-selling-novel *The Virginian* (1902). That landmark work of fiction proved to be a perfect Janus symbol, looking backward to invoke the frontier images of the nineteenth century, facing forward as a model for thousands of fictional treatments of the West in the next fifty years.

Meanwhile, other voices and stories were overlooked or omitted that could have enriched and diversified the metanarrative of the American West. For example, even though the female population nearly equalled the number of men living in or immigrating to the West in the last years of the nineteenth century, their lives and experiences rarely became the central focus of fiction or histories about the frontier. If their stories were told, they were usually straitjacketed into acceptable formulas or quickly forgotten.

The notable woman novelist and artist Mary Hallock Foote, for instance, pictured a much milder, more domestic West than dime novelists or Local Color writers depicted in the Gilded Age. Even though her work attracted a good deal of attention before the turn of the century, her portraits of women and families in a newly settled West were swept aside in the next decades in a flood of popular novels and films about a wild, masculine frontier. In another case, the story of Martha Canary/Calamity Jane became overnight a familiar Wild West narrative in which she could out shoot, out swear, and out drink "the rest of the boys." In the earliest accounts of Calamity, her role as an independent—and tragic—pioneer woman was quickly lost beneath the sensational and distorted accounts of her life.

Much the same happened to stories by Native Americans. Not until the 1920s and 1930s did the first crop of Native American warrior narratives tell their divergent side of a closing frontier. As often as not, too, these autobiographical accounts were of the "told to" variety such as Black Elk's story through John Neihardt or the narratives of Pretty-shield and Plenty-coups through Frank Linderman. Unfortunately, these stories came too late to change notably the western story. By the mid-1920s, this story line had hardened into a veritable formula, in which Indians play the role of opponents, the Other, against whom masculine white heroes test their courage and endurance.[1]

The story of Geronimo and its first appearances in print illuminate the exclusionary power of the Wild West story. That narrative accepted no revisions and thus refused to incorporate Geronimo's perspective as part of a revised, enlarged story. Yet Geronimo's experiences suggest what the western story might have become had his and other Native voices been heard and accepted soon after the turn of the century.[2]

An even more poignant example of the elided Native American story surfaces in one of the first novels by an Indian woman. *Cogewea: The Half-Blood* by Mourning Dove (Hum-ishu-ma), or Christine Quintasket, illustrates the dilemmas an author faced in trying to write a novel with an Indian perspective, but also one structured within the strictures of a frontier cowboy story. Although an obviously flawed work of literature, the novel nonetheless reveals the cultural barriers that surrounded and helped determine the form and content of the western narrative in the first decades of the twentieth century.[3]

MARY HALLOCK FOOTE came west in 1876, a new bride from upstate New York, half expecting to stay for only a few months on a raw frontier. She hoped to enjoy her brief lark in California but planned to return soon to her sociocultural havens in New York state. None of these dreams worked out. For most of the next half-century, Mary Foote followed her diligent but unsuccessful engineer husband, Arthur Foote, from California, to Colorado, to Idaho, and back to California. All the while she yearned to retreat east to her family along the Hudson and to her lifelong friend Helena deKay Gilder in New York City. Homesick, frustrated, and sometimes nearly distraught, Mary felt an alien in a strange land during her first two decades in the pioneer West. A move to Grass Valley, California, in the late 1890s and with it a dependable position for Arthur, however, finally brought a measure of acceptance and satisfaction. During the next quarter-century, Foote achieved something of an "angle of repose" in her life.[4]

In her first two decades in the West, however, Foote suffered through several traumatic experiences. At first she hoped to build upon her considerable training and success as an illustrator. Those hopes, although partially realized, were increasingly frustrated. The pressures of motherhood (her first child, Arthur, came in 1877; her second, Betty, in 1882; and there were miscarriages); Arthur's inability to land and keep a remunerative position; and Molly's numerous worries about health, finances, and isolation from family and friends kept her on edge. Far from her patrons and models, a cultured middle-class woman forced to live in mining camps and isolated cabins, and lacking the time to execute her wood-block art, Mary had mounting difficulty trying to balance her life as wife and mother and as artist.[5]

Meanwhile, she found unexpected outlets for her artistic energies. Her newsy and descriptive personal letters from the Far West so entertained Helena and her well-known husband, Richard Watson Gilder, editor of *Century Magazine,* that they encouraged Molly to write for publication. Expressing numerous misgivings, Foote nonetheless began to produce essays and stories in the late 1870s and early 1880s. Although Mary retired from her artwork by the turn of the century, from the 1870s until the eve of World War I, she turned out dozens of sketches, short stories, serials, and novels focused primarily on the nineteenth-century American West.[6]

In most of her writing, Foote portrayed engineers, miners, farmers, and families rather than the newly popular cowboy, Indian, and frontier military subjects that dominated the paintings and fiction of such contemporary artists and authors as Frederic Remington, Charles Russell, and Owen Wister. In doing so, Foote supplied a notable alternative to the story of a Wild West. Her Local Color stories, often with her own illustrations, furnished appealing portraits of a domestic West, frequently emphasizing women and families.[7]

Foote's domestic West revealingly bears little resemblance to some recent rereadings of the western past. For one, she accepted and participated in the patriarchal society to which she was born and in which she matured. She seemed most uncomfortable when circumstances forced her out of the daughter-wife-mother roles she most preferred. When Arthur was unable to support their growing family, she had to turn out several serials, short stories, and paintings to make "the pot boil," as she said. Still, even though Foote fretted about betraying her traditional and comfortable roles as wife and mother, she never wavered from her conviction that women's and family concerns should be the central emphases in her fiction and art. In fact, throughout her career, Mary Hallock Foote filled her personal correspondence, her stories and novels, and her illustrations with dozens of provocative and illuminating portraits of women and families. From the very beginning she depicted a domestic West greatly at odds from the Wests of Buffalo Bill and the dime novelists.[8]

Foote's first novel *The Led-Horse Claim* (1883) clearly illustrates how her fiction differed from Wild West stories and the work of other Local Color writers. Here Foote focuses on mining camp life in the northern Rockies, where she had lived. Although the novel opens with a conflict between two mining operations, it treats primarily the romantic story of Cecil Conrath, the sister of one of the mine managers, and George Hilgard, the competing operator. Much of the story is seen through the heroine's perspective, most of the supporting characters are female, and a large share of the friendships are among women. Nothing in this novel resembles the competitive, male, test-of-courage narrative of the Wild West shows and dime novels.[9]

Although many frontier mining camps were overwhelmingly masculine in numbers and social patterns, Foote devotes large attention to women in her novel. For several of these females, mining camp experiences are particularly traumatic. One of the women, Mrs. Derry, described as "a lively little matron, whose six months' residence in the camp made her a veteran in its society" (45), relieves her boredom through flirtation. Another young woman says: "It is a woman's place always to make peace, but [in this camp] it has been useless to try" (104). Still another young woman who "came from the East ten years ago," now "exhibited a rather weather-beaten fairness"; she "has had a beautiful time, but she begins to show it a little" (48, 49). In fact, so hungry are the women for friendship that in one mining camp house, class distinctions crumble: "Mistress and maid, living so near together, and being of nearly the same age, did not pretend to a very formal relation" (132). Attempting to overcome the palpable isolation and evident social needs, "every house over which a woman presided practiced a hospitality out of all proportion, in its scope, to the capacities of the rude tabernacle" (13–14).

The heroine feels adrift in the mining camp West. A pretty young woman raised without much parental attention, Cecil comes to the Rockies to visit her brother Conrad. But isolated from the nearby town and unable to see much of her brother, she is frequently alone and betrays her alienation from her surroundings. On one occasion, when horrified with threatened violence, Cecil stutters out her emotional reactions. To which Mrs. Derry replies: "You would n't make a good miner's wife, Cecil" (122). When her brother is shot in an underground squabble, perhaps by Hilgard to whom she is attracted, she flees east to abandon an uncivilized West.

Even though Foote's excessive use of chance and circumstance to satisfy her editor's demands mar the novel's ending, she nonetheless provides a clearcut image of the mining camp West. That frontier often separates families, it is hard on cultivated women, and for young women without strong family ties it can be a hellish place. The heroine's grandmother may be voicing and commenting on Foote's own experiences when she says of Cecil's West: "It was no place for a young girl." Then she adds: "When people went West . . . when I was a girl . . . they thought about it beforehand; they consulted their friends; families went together. They were a long while going, and when they got there, they stayed. There was none of this rushing back and forth, thousands of miles at a stretch" (271)!

The Last Assembly Ball (1889), a later novel, reveals how much Foote wished to make distinctions between East and West and how much she was intrigued with class divisions. The plot of this quickly written novel deserves but brief attention. It is the trite story of a easterner, Frank Embury, fleeing west to escape a disappointed love and his unfortunate fall, almost overnight, for a servant girl in the West, Milly Robinson, who has a flawed past. His love on the rebound and her inability to explain an earlier marriage and motherhood lead to a tragic ending. It is for other reasons, not the story line, that this novel merits comment.[10]

In several of Foote's early sketches and stories she embedded, almost as cultural asides, brief comparisons between the American East and West. But in *The Last Assembly Ball,* these regional contrasts, particularly when tied to gender, family, and class relationships, underlie the entire story. In fact, the four-page "Introductory" discloses false eastern assumptions about the West even as it lays out the nature of western history and society. "Among . . . unsafe assumptions," Foote begins, "the East has decided that nothing can be freer and simpler than the social life of the far West, exemplified by the flannel shirt and the flowing necktie, the absence of polish on boots and manners." That point of view is misguided, Foote continues, because "as a matter of experience, no society is so puzzling in its relations, so exacting in its demands upon self-restraint, as one which has no methods, which is yet in the stage of fermentation" (5). That is the stage of social development in the West, and the East has misread western development.

One of the major female characters in the novel, a widowed landlady Fanny Danksen, pictures East-West differences in marital terms. "Eastern women may be wanted in the West," she asserts, "but Western women are never wanted in the East. Why? Because there are women enough there already—women who are acclimated, body and soul. And how does it end? You forsake your East for the sake of your wife, or your wife for the sake of your East" (33–34)! The narrator speaks with equal certainty a few pages later when she states: "When an Eastern woman goes West, she parts at one wrench with family, clan, traditions, clique, cult, and all that has hitherto enabled her to merge her outlines." But once in the West, she loses her connections, her definitional ties in "the arid light of a new community, where there are no traditions and no backgrounds. Her angles are all discovered, but none of her affinities" (39–40).

These comments are particularly revealing because they so closely parallel what Mary Hallock Foote experienced in the West. She too worried about how the Far West would shape her life. The move to Idaho in the mid-1880s, she wrote, "meant farewell [to] music, art, gossip of the workshop, schools that we knew about, new friends just made who would forget us, old friends better loved than ever and harder to part from—all the old backgrounds receding hopelessly and forever."[11] And, after persons have been in the West for a space of time, people whom the narrator types as a "tenderfoot," they are still "femininely speaking, between a past not yet abandoned and a present reluctantly accepted."[12] Those sentiments encapsulated what Foote had written two years earlier in one of her most revealing letters to Helena Gilder:

> It occurred to me that there is a class of Americans not yet classified—strangers in their native land, exiles under their own flag—the relations of these people with other exiles, with the natives they happen to be thrown with, their semi-estrangement from the West—their pride and their despair in the life they lead—their restlessness and their longing for rest—their disaffection and their loyalty seem to me an interesting side of American life. . . . The most bewildering thought is that perhaps we belong to this unclassified class ourselves. What if we should find that we cannot live East because we have lived too long in the West.[13]

In echoing several themes explicit in her fiction, dozens of Mary Hallock Foote's illustrations substantiate her position as an exception to the familiar ingredients of the Wild West story. A graduate of the Cooper Institute School of Design for Women, Foote had already completed, while in her twenties, woodblock illustrations of eastern rural scenes as well as others for notable authors Henry Wadsworth Longfellow, Nathaniel Hawthorne, John Greenleaf Whittier, and Alfred Lord Tennyson. Then, in the late 1870s she began to illustrate her own sketches and stories. These picturesque illustrations of California mining camps, and of Mexico in the early 1880s (the Footes made a brief trip to Mexico in 1881), are superb examples of Local Color art. Some admiringly depict local scenes, dress, and social activities. Others are romantic portraits of California coastal towns and Mexican haciendas, including many positive portraits of provincial character types.[14]

But new responsibilities as a wife and mother in isolated spots of the West made it increasingly difficult for Foote to continue her work as a nationally recognized illustrator. Without the live models she wanted and the research costumes she needed for her work, Foote declined to illustrate the works of other

Mary Hallock Foote, *The Orchard Wind-Break* (1889)

Mary Hallock Foote's illustrations frequently featured women as nurturers, as middle ground figures between nature and settlement. Mary Hallock Foote, *The Orchard Wind-Break, Century Magazine* 38 (February 1889): 501.

writers. Besides, her many moves and the financial uncertainties of her family weighed on her. She then decided to illustrate only her own work.

The six illustrations she prepared for *The Led-Horse Claim* foreshadow the emphases of her artwork during the next decade. The first illustration, *At the Foot of the Pass,* limns the gigantic Rockies confronting those who wish to enter the mining camp setting. Two of the other woodcuts depict the heroine in stressful moods; another portrays her and the hero trying to make an important decision. The hero and his assistant manager ponder the future of their mine in *The Led-Horse in Council.* The final illustration, *Cecil's Ring,* shows a latecomer to the mining camp discovering the heroine's ring, which the protagonist had lost soon after Cecil gave it to him as a pledge of her feelings. Interestingly, in the text Foote identifies the ring as "presumptive proof of civilized feminine occupation at an early period of the Shoshone [mine] history" (277). All of these artworks represent Foote's depiction of the West as something other than a violent place. Although her novel includes at least one explicitly violent scene and the suggestion of others, none of Foote's illustrations portrays the West as the site of turbulent confrontations. Nothing smacks of a Wild West.

The most significant collection of Foote's illustrations are the eleven sketches of the Far West series. Published in monthly installments in *Century Magazine* in 1888–89 and accompanied by brief explanatory texts that Foote also prepared, the series remains quite simply the most revealing clutch of illustrations by a woman of the late nineteenth-century West.[15]

Several works in the series deal with traditional pioneer subjects, but even in these illustrations Foote undercuts Wild West images of an exuberant, adventuresome, even violence-prone frontier. The returning hunter in *Looking for Camp,* the wandering herdsmen and barren landscapes in *The Choice of Reuben and Gad,* the hardworking teamsters in *The Last Trip In,* and the laborer waiting for work in *The Winter Camp—A Day's Ride from the Mail—* all these frontiersmen are presented in muted, flat, nearly tamed terms. Even in *The Sheriff's Posse* the riders "make haste slowly," often tracking not a dangerous criminal but a cowboy who has wounded a sheepherder he considers an interloper. Almost as an aside, Foote admits she has "never yet encountered anything so sensational as a troop of armed men on the track of a criminal" (272).

The remainder of the paintings evoke Mary Hallock Foote's domestic West. In *Afternoon at a Ranch* and *The Pretty Girls in the West* the artist uses her home up the Boise Canyon for portraits of girls or of young girls courting. In *The Coming of Winter*, a madonnalike pioneer wife holding her baby balances a scene in which her rifle-carrying husband seems ready to fire his weapon. The woman riding side-saddle in *Cinching Up* also furnishes a feminine touch to that scene.

The remaining sketches, *The Orchard Wind-Break* and *The Irrigating Ditch*, two superb illustrations, wonderfully illustrate Foote's mild West. In the first of the two paintings, a very attractive young woman in a white apron stands near a young fawn who seems to be nuzzling the woman's breast. Behind and beside the woman, an orchard windbreak and an irrigation ditch magnify her image as a civilizer. But because she touches the deer as well as represents cultivation, she occupies a middle ground, a nurturing link between nature and society.

The Irrigating Ditch is freighted with even larger meanings. Another one of Foote's madonna figures stands quietly holding her baby near an irrigating ditch. The surrounding tall trees and verdant grasses merge with the mother to produce a scene of fruitfulness and placidity. In the accompanying text, Foote's metaphor links symbol and idea. She writes: "each freshly plowed field that encroaches upon the aboriginal sage-brush is a new stitch taken in the pattern of civilization which runs, a slender, bright border, along the skirt of the desert's dusty garment" (287).

More than most of Foote's illustrations, *The Engineer's Mate* (1895) draws revealing comparisons between East and West. A stylishly dressed (eastern?) young woman stands alone on an isolated (western) railroad platform. Her sophisticated attire and her large pile of luggage contrast with the open, spare surrounding landscape. The contrasts in the scene remind one of Foote's description of the railroad station at Kuna, where she had disembarked after her first reluctant trip to Idaho a decade earlier. "No one remembers Kuna," she writes. "It was a place where silence closed about you after the bustle of the train, where a soft, dry wind from great distances hummed through the telegraph wires and a stage road went out of sight in one direction and a new railroad track in another." The wind "came across immense dry areas without an object to harp upon except the man-made wires. There was not a tree in sight— miles and miles of pallid sagebrush."[16]

The artist implies several disjunctures between the eastern, genteel woman and the unsettled, uncultivated West. Although Foote had spent most of the previous two decades in California, Colorado, and Idaho before executing this

Mary Hallock Foote, *The Engineer's Mate* (1895)

Mary Hallock Foote's woodcut artwork represented a domestic West that lost out in the twentieth century to dominant male stories of a Wild West. Mary Hallock Foote, *The Engineer's Mate*, *Century Magazine* 50 (May 1895): 90.

artwork, its contents and her private correspondence indicate how much her heart remained in the East. Rather than paint a lively, fun-loving West, she considered it, especially many of the Boiseans she had met during the last decade, as provincial, if not socially inferior.[17]

A final painting, *Between the Desert and the Sown,* although not Foote's best work, nonetheless exudes cultural meaning. As in several of the artist's other illustrations, an irrigation canal full to the brim divides the painting into two competing halves. Above the ditch, cramped into the right-hand corner, a lone mounted cowboy stirs up dust as he gallops through arid country. Below the canal on its lower bank, a well-dressed young woman serenely surveys the irrigated country and settlements that sweep before her to the mountains on the horizon. Foote clearly identifies the young woman with fructiveness, settlement, and civilization, whereas the male figure is associated with a stern, uncultivated desert. As she did so often in her fiction, and in other illustrations as well, Foote links female figures, once in the West, with society, civilization, and gentility—in opposition to a masculine, raw, and new frontier.[18]

Even before Foote's novel *Between the Desert and Sown* was published in 1902, the same year Wister's *The Virginian* appeared, her life seemed to reach a tentative angle of repose. After the publication of that novel, now that the Foote family was situated in Grass Valley, California, that her husband had a steady, good-paying job, and that her children were adults or adolescents, Mary found less to worry about, less to fight, less to quarrel with in the West. That growing sense of satisfaction seeps in around the edges of her fiction. Rather than depict an East of tradition at odds with a nascent West, Foote turned to other less anguished subjects. In these later novels, parents worry about their maturing children and their choices of mates, and in *The Royal Americans* (1910) and *The Picked Company* (1912) Foote produced her first historical novels, works quite remote in context and mood from her fiction of the 1880s and 1890s.

But in the first two decades of her literary career, from the publication of her first novel in 1882 until the appearance of *Between the Desert and the Sown,* Mary Hallock Foote pictured a West distinct from that popular in Wild West stories. In her emphases on East-West sociocultural conflicts, in her stress on gender relations, in her depiction of class tensions, and particularly in her concentration on a domestic West, she offered subjects different from those in contemporary dime novels and Local Color stories. The absence of these topics in many Westerns in the first half of the twentieth century evidences the limited influences of Mary Hallock Foote and like-minded writers on the developing western story. The paucity of those materials narrowed the focus of many Westerns, fictional and cinematic, in the next fifty years.

In NEARLY EVERY WAY, Martha Canary/Calamity Jane differed from Mary Hallock Foote. Their backgrounds, their roles as pioneer women, and their significance as cultural figures in the West are as divergent as one could imagine. Yet in one respect they were similar. Neither of their personal narratives became an important ingredient in the western story. If Foote's domestic West was omitted, Calamity's role as an independent frontierswoman was transformed, distorted, and stylized to meet the needs of the Wild West narrative.[19]

Martha Canary/Calamity Jane remains the mystery figure of the major Wild West characters. All of the other demigods like General George Custer, Buffalo Bill Cody, Wild Bill Hickok, Billy the Kid, Annie Oakley, Belle Starr, and such Indian leaders as Crazy Horse, Sitting Bull, and Geronimo have been the subject of a thoroughly researched, modern biography. Not Calamity. Only a few general details are known about her life.[20]

On the other hand, enough of those details are available to see how she became something different in legends and popular culture than she was in life. Born in 1856, the daughter of a lethargic Missouri farmer Robert Canary and his promiscuous wife Charlotte, Martha retreated farther west with her parents after their unsuccessful attempts at farming in northern Missouri and southern Iowa. Evidently hoping to strike a bonanza in a frontier mining camp, the Canary family, with their three or four children, took the trail to the booming strikes in the West in the early 1860s.[21]

Rather than riches, the Canarys experienced disappointments, decline, and, eventually, tragedy. A brief story in *The Montana Post* at the end of 1864 provided one revealing glimpse of how quickly the family had succumbed to the vicissitudes of boom and bust of so many frontier mining extravaganzas. A journalist reported that three young girls, one a mere babe in arms, by the name of Canary had appeared at the home of one of the community's commissioners. On a bitterly cold day they were dressed in the scantiest of clothing and they were hungry. They asked for and received food and clothing. Toward the end of his pathetic story, the reporter referred to the girls' father as a gambler and their mother as "a woman of the lowest grade."[22] Destitution soon cycled further downward. In 1866, Charlotte died in Blackfoot City, Montana, and the next year, after retreating to Salt Lake City with his young children, Robert also died. At the age of eleven, Martha was an orphan, without family, community, or any means of support.

Even before Martha became a teenager, her life impressively diverged from that of most young girls in the West. Lacking parents, an extended family, a church, or any other nurturing institution or community to guide her through her adolescent years, she became something of a social waif. She was at the mercy of those willing to take on a girl who, undoubtedly, had experience much beyond her years. But the stories of these traumas and the scars of these early years never appeared in the later overblown accounts of Calamity Jane as the premier Wild Woman of the West.

Calamity Jane, Wild Westerner

Martha Canary ("Calamity Jane") was often depicted as a masculine character, even though she wished to be an independent pioneer woman. (Courtesy of the American Heritage Center, University of Wyoming)

Chapter Two

The next few years of Martha's life are a jumble of rumors and yarns, thrown together in an uncertain mix that refuses to gel into a clear pattern. In an often untrustworthy autobiography, ghost-written or dictated nearly forty years later, Martha/Calamity says she spent the next few years in western Wyoming, at Ft. Bridger, Piedmont, and other nearby forts and railroad towns. Fortunately, a territorial census of 1869 locates her in Piedmont, and stories taken from oldtimers a half-century later confirm that she lived for short periods in the boom-and-bust hamlets of Piedmont, Atlantic City, and Miners' Delight in southwestern Wyoming. Martha, it was said, worked as a baby-sitter, as a waitress, and a cleaning girl. But without an education (she was probably illiterate), occupational training or experience, or a family on which to rely, the teenage Martha was adrift, floating from fort, to railroad hamlet, to jerrybuilt new towns.[23]

Sometime in the mid-1870s, perhaps in 1875, Martha became Calamity Jane. Although she said her new name came from her rescue of an injured army man, it is more likely that her unorthodox, even alienating behavior resulted in the new nickname. When young women were expected to be daughters until they married young and soon became mothers, Calamity Jane was already shocking observers with her smoking, chewing, swearing, drinking, and, possibly, sexual abandon. At any rate, Calamity she became, and once christened that, Martha Canary disappeared. Few in the next century and more knew her real name or her early lifestory.

Between 1875 and 1878, in a series of dramatic steps, Calamity Jane vaulted onto center stage of an emerging Wild West. In 1875 she tagged along with the expedition of Walter P. Jenny and Colonel R. T. Dodge to scout out the Black Hills. A year later she joined General George Crook's troops as they marched north to do battle with the Sioux. Chased out of both expeditions as a possible camp follower, Calamity may have returned a second time with Crook in the late spring of 1876. But the most historic of her escapades came in June and July of 1876. As General Custer marched toward his doom at the Little Big Horn in eastern Montana, Calamity, recently released from jail in Cheyenne, cavorted northward to Ft. Laramie. A few days later she joined Wild Bill Hickok and a handful of comrades on a quick journey to the Black Hills. In July, the group, dressed in new buckskins, paraded into Deadwood, creating an impression that still shaped memories decades later.[24]

By summer's end, Calamity's reputation had spread throughout the interior northern West. A year later, newspapermen were comparing the twenty-one-year old to a vivacious if controversial Bret Harte heroine. These stories were likely based on a few newspaper details and a brief profile of Calamity in H. N. Maguire's *The Black Hills and American Wonderland* (1877), a popular work by a South Dakota journalist that appeared serially in a New York paper. Several similar phrases and mistaken facts from the newspapers and Maguire's account reappeared in the first dime novel about Calamity, Edward Wheeler's *Deadwood Dick, the Prince of the Road; or, The Black Rider of the Black Hills* (October 15, 1877). Within a few months, Calamity, described as "an original in herself," as an "uneducated, uncared for" young woman, also played a major role in T. M. Newson's play *Drama of Life in the Black Hills* (1878).[25]

This sudden and widespread publicity meant that Calamity had become at twenty-two a well-known woman of the Wild West. Although writers frequently depicted Calamity as dressing like a man and as having lived "a rough and dissipated" life, they had to admit that these rigors had not "altogether 'swept away the lines where beauty lingers.'"[26] In Wheeler's several dime novels, for example, Calamity rides, shoots, and scraps with the toughest frontier owlhoots, yet her alabaster-white upper neck and arms retain their loveliness. Here and elsewhere, Calamity is reputed to have been seduced and ruined at an early age, forcing her into a lonely, nontraditional life for a woman.

In these years of high emotionalism about a Wild West, Calamity had surfaced as a devil-may-care young woman worthy of mention alongside Buffalo Bill, Billy the Kid, and Wild Bill Hickok. Indeed, Calamity's apotheosis occurred during the five years between Custer's demise and Hickok's assassination in the summer of 1876 and Billy's death and the Shootout at the OK Corral in 1881. Introduced to readers as a she-cat of a violent and tumultuous Old West, Calamity was stylized not as an independent pioneer woman but as a female hellion who should be considered "one of the boys."

For most of Calamity's remaining years until her death in 1903, she was portrayed in newspapers and other mediums as a Wild West character. If she drifted from forts to railroad towns to mining camps in her first two decades in Wyoming and western South Dakota, she rambled through a series of new ranch and farm and railroad towns primarily in central and southern Wyoming and southern and eastern Montana in the 1880s and 1890s. In many of those years, reporters in Rawlins and Lander, Wyoming, and in Miles City, Billings, and Livingston, Montana, delighted in telling of Calamity's latest drinking rumbles, often landing her in a local jail for a night or two. National publications, picking up on these images emerging from the West, also depicted Calamity Jane as a Wild West Woman.[27]

These dramatic images of Calamity as a well-known frontier figure helped lead to her participation in three shows. In the mid-1880s she traveled for a few days with the Hardwick show, which unfortunately was unable to pay its performers and so quickly disbanded. Then, a decade later, in early 1896, Calamity signed on with the Kohl-Middleton traveling troupe to take part in their performances for dime museums. Advertising for Calamity's role in this organization demonstrates how much she had become stereotyped as a female terror of a fabulous frontier. A handbill and a newspaper come-on for a presentation in Minneapolis depicted her as a western Amazon dressed in ragged buckskins with a vicious knife clenched between her teeth. The caption described Calamity as "The Famous Woman Scout of the Wild West! Heroine of a Thousand Adventures! Terror of Evildoers in the Black Hills! The Comrade of Buffalo Bill and Wild Bill!" More exaggeration and falsehood than truth, this sensational billing paralleled the stretchers and lies about Calamity appearing in contemporary fiction and journalistic stories. Before long, Calamity was out of the troupe and soon back in Deadwood. Without a job or family for support, Calamity wandered throughout Montana and adjacent states attempting to sell her photograph and her seven-page autobiography cobbled together for appearances with Kohl and Middleton. With little or no income, Calamity was poverty stricken, depressed, and sick, dependent on others for food and a place to stay. She verged on complete destitution.[28]

Then another striking series of circumstances promised her financial and personal security. A New York writer, Josephine Brake, came to Montana to rescue Calamity from her destitution—and with the possible additional motive of using the Wild West heroine to sell Brake's books. Taking Calamity east to Buffalo to participate in the Pan-American Exposition, Brake promised to underwrite all of Calamity's needs. Not surprisingly, Calamity soon tired of hawking Brake's books and joined Col. Frederic Cummins's Great Indian Congress, then in Buffalo, where she was billed as a famous frontier figure. Discontent and alcohol, often a disastrous mixture, unhorsed Calamity. Penniless, she was unable to return west until Buffalo Bill purchased a train ticket for her.[29]

After Calamity slunk back west, she seemed to lose her will to live. Increasingly, she wobbled from place to place, unable to keep a job and to avoid drinking binges. During one of her moments of depression, Calamity reportedly told her Montana cowboy friend Teddy Blue, "Why don't the sons of bitches leave me alone and let me go to hell on my own route?" That end came quickly after a series of debilitating sprees in the spring and summer of 1903. She died in Terry, South Dakota, on August 1, 1903, and was buried three days later next to Wild Bill Hickok in Mt. Moriah Cemetery in Deadwood. Even at her funeral, which several hundreds attended, Calamity was lionized as a lively, adventurous hellcat of the Wild West.[30]

It is not surprising that early on Calamity became a resident of the pantheon of Wild West heroes and heroines. An orphan before she became a teenager, coming to adulthood among predominantly male populations at forts, jerry-built railroad hamlets, and mining boomtowns, Calamity grew up among soldiers, miners, and other frontiersmen. Her exploits as rider, as a person of daring and courage, as an antisocial woman known for her drinking and swearing gained her companions largely among men, not with women. Once her unorthodox actions became known and were recorded in newspapers, histories, and dime novels, she was transformed into Calamity Jane, a Wild Woman of a Wild West.

But another kind of person evolved from Martha Canary, one little known and quite different from the stereotyped wildcat Calamity Jane. This independent woman of the frontier West relished her family, wanted to be married, loved children, and dressed like and desired to be a typical pioneer woman. In her brief autobiography, Calamity says she was the oldest of six children. Only two of these siblings can be traced to adulthood, her younger sister Lena and her younger brother Elijah (Lije). Three years younger than Martha, Lena as a teenager married a German immigrant, John Borner (Boerner).[31] They settled near Lander, Wyoming, and Calamity, by several accounts, visited her sister as often as she could elude her brother-in-law, who thought of her as a wild, immoral woman. Although Calamity rarely saw Lije, she felt a close bond with him. On one occasion, a Montana miner and former prisoner told Calamity he had been in southwestern Wyoming and had recently seen Elijah (Lije had just been released from the Wyoming Territorial Prison after serving most of a five-year sentence for obstructing a railroad and filing false damages). When he told Calamity of his meeting with Lije, she "broke down and sobbed like a child." He added that in the emotion of hearing about "her 'baby' brother, that being the pet name she had . . . bestowed upon him," she forced a present on the miner. In other accounts, Tobe Borner, Calamity's nephew, frequently referred to the affection Calamity felt for her family.[32]

Calamity Jane, Independent Pioneer Woman

Calamity Jane's role as an independent pioneer woman frequently disappeared under an avalanche of purple prose depicting her as "one of the boys" in western stories. (Courtesy of the American Heritage Center, University of Wyoming)

Calamity also became a mother, giving birth to at least one son and one daughter. In the early 1880s Montana newspapers reported that she had borne a son whom she called "Little Calamity." Later sources mention the baby, but he evidently died very young. In June 1887, another journalist described Calamity as "in a rather delicate condition."[33] Four months afterwards, she became the mother of a little girl. Off and on up to her death, Calamity had custody of her daughter and often spoke of trying to find work or financial help to support the girl. Others who knew Calamity commented frequently on how much she loved and doted on children. Conversely, the best evidence proves that Calamity was not the mother of Jean Hickok McCormick, who claimed to be the love offspring of Calamity and Wild Bill Hickok. Equally spurious were McCormick's claims that a diary in her possession belonged to Calamity and included entries and letters written to Jean ("Dear Janey") in the last decades of Calamity's life.[34] Although Calamity never married Wild Bill, nor was he her sweetheart, she immensely enjoyed the company of men. She even claimed several as her "husband." In interviews, Calamity spoke often of her mates, suggesting that she much desired to be a wife and mother. During the 1880s she called herself Mrs. Mattie King, and in 1886 referred to William Steers as her husband. Probably Steers fathered her daughter who was born in 1887. And from a recently discovered document, we now know that Calamity and Steers were in southeastern Idaho in 1888 and were officially married.[35] Calamity also spoke repeatedly of Clinton Burke as her husband; they may have even operated a boarding house in the early 1890s. Finally, in the later 1890s, after Burke disappeared, Calamity claimed Robert Dorsett as her new husband. Only Steers is known to be her legal husband, after two children were born. Yet Calamity seemed to want respectability, to be a pioneer wife, to be accepted as such, and thus often represented herself as a married woman.

An important interview in the mid-1890s reveals how much Calamity wanted to be viewed as a typical pioneer wife. When a journalist found her at home, she fretted about her unruly hair and her untidy home. With Calamity was her "husband" and her daughter Jessie. She told the interviewer that she was ashamed of some of her past deeds and hoped now to make a comfortable home for her family. The reporter surmised what few biographers and even more western storytellers have not realized: most of all, Calamity desired to be a wife and mother, to be like other women.[36] Regrettably, the human, even domestic side of Calamity remains hidden behind hundreds of sensational and stereotyped stories about her unorthodox actions as a Wild West hellcat.

The same mistaken notions arise from photographs of Calamity. When historians mention Calamity in their western stories, she is usually depicted as wearing buckskins. If only one photograph is utilized in these accounts, she almost always is shown in men's attire. Such representations are misleading. In the more than two dozen extant photographs, Calamity is usually dressed in typical late nineteenth-century women's clothing. Most often, she is wearing floor-length dresses, usually black or another dark color. Occasionally she is dressed in a mix-match, light-and-dark skirt and blouse. Sometimes a long apron covers her shoetop-length skirt. When contemporary journalists or other writers mention meeting Calamity on the street, she is described as wearing women's clothes. Nearly always, when dressed in buckskins or men's clothing, Calamity was accompanying the troops, posing for a stock photograph, or taking part in a Wild West extravaganza.[37] Again, popular representations distort her image as a pioneer woman, turning her instead into "one of the boys."

The stories by which Calamity Jane's image was formulated and packaged illustrate what happened to other western women of similar controversial actions and unorthodox character. For Calamity, as for Belle Starr, Cattle Kate, Pearl Hart, and even Annie Oakley, their lives as frontier females were frequently forced into the mold of a rootin' tootin' Wild West woman. Their experiences as wives, mothers, and family members were sublimated to the needs of a frontier formula. If Mary Hallock Foote's domestic West was omitted or overlooked because it failed to fit the specifics of the Wild West narrative, Calamity Jane's life was denatured, her role as a pioneer woman neutered so that she might be imagined as an acceptable sidekick figure for Wild Bill Hickok or the likes of Buffalo Bill Cody, Billy the Kid, or Wyatt Earp.

So powerful were these homogenizing influences that Calamity Jane's role as a Wild West figure has persisted well into the twentieth century. In most of this century, she has appeared as a female outlaw or gunslinger, sometimes as Wild Bill's consort as in *The Plainsman* (1936), or in the form-fitting buckskins of tomboy Doris Day in the later movie *Calamity Jane* (1953). Not until the 1980s have movie makers (e.g., Jane Alexander in *Calamity Jane,* 1984) and novelists (Pete Dexter, *Deadwood,* 1986; and Larry McMurtry, *Buffalo Girls,* 1990) begun to depict Calamity as a gray heroine of complex and ambiguous identity. Yet even these later revisionists have done little with her as a pioneer woman, except to depict her incorrectly as the mother of Jean Hickok McCormick. Still, perhaps these recent attempts at revising the Wild West story will encourage other writers and directors to discover Calamity Jane as an independent woman of the pioneer West. One wonders what course the western story might have taken if early on lively, nonconformist females such as Calamity had been treated as important characters on their own rather than as women subordinated to the needs of a patriarchal western narrative.[38]

THE voices of Native Americans central to the history of the trans-Mississippi American West in the late nineteenth century suffered a fate similar to many women's experiences of the same period. The western story did not allot space for Indians' narratives of their experiences in the three or four decades following the Civil War. Instead they were forced into the role of "savage" Opponents. Competitions with Indians became tests for white male courage and bravery. That meant, by and large, Indian stories were not heard in the Gilded Age and that many of the Indian-white conflict stories would not appear until the 1920s and 1930s, well after the western story had hardened into a clearly recognized, predictable narrative. That Indian accounts of contention with whites were not recognized in the decades surrounding 1900 reveals much about American cultural currents of that time.[39]

None of the best-known *western* Indian leaders published a full-scale autobiography during the nineteenth century. Although Sitting Bull provided "pictographic" accounts of his actions after his capture, neither he nor Crazy Horse prepared or dictated the stories of their lives before their deaths. If these victors at the Little Big Horn in 1876 left no life stories, the valiant Chief Joseph, whose nearly successful and courageous retreat the next year won the hearts of many Americans, provided a few comments about his actions. Published as "An Indian's Views of Indian Affairs" in 1879 in the *North American Review* and later retitled "Chief Joseph's Own Story," it was a translated speech dealing more with policy than with his own life.[40] In the last part of the nineteenth century most American writers and readers seemed more interested in treating Indians as barbarians or as childlike and in need of civilizing rather than as possible authors of their own western stories.

Two works by Native Americans in the first decades of the twentieth century illustrate Indian perspectives that could have leavened the Wild West story. They also represent the difficulties in treating these books as entirely authentic works by Native Americans. Despite these persisting dilemmas for cultural interpreters, these two volumes, like the writings and artwork of Mary Hallock Foote and the images of Calamity Jane, tell us much about other stories that failed to become part of the Wild West narrative during the authors' lifetimes.

Geronimo's Story of His Life (1906), as "taken down and edited by S. M. Barrett," is the only full-length narrative by one of the major Indian warriors to be published before the 1920s. As an experienced frontiersman, as a person well acquainted with Indians, and as superintendent of schools in Lawton, Oklahoma, Stephen Melvil Barrett had become acquainted with Geronimo, then a prisoner of war in nearby Ft. Sill. A few brief conversations in 1904 and 1905 with the Apache war leader and shaman encouraged Barrett to ask if he could publish some of Geronimo's oral stories. In Geronimo's nearly twenty years of captivity (he had finally surrendered to General Nelson Miles in 1886), he had learned the white man's fascination with money, so he told Barrett he would tell his full story for a fee if the schoolman could secure permission for the project from army officers. Those in charge at Ft. Sill refused, asserting that because of "the many depredations committed by Geronimo and his warriors . . . the old Apache deserved to be hanged rather than spoiled by so much attention." But an appeal to President Theodore Roosevelt, who was interested in Indians and whom Geronimo had met during Roosevelt's inaugural festivities in 1905, opened the way for Barrett to give Geronimo "a chance to tell his side of the story."[41]

Barrett then worked out the details of the collaboration. Because he could not converse directly with Geronimo and because the Apache spoke little English, Asa Daklugie, Geronimo's second cousin and the son of Whoa (Juh), served as translator. Geronimo refused to speak in the presence of a transcriber. Rather, he talked each day of what interested him, told Daklugie and Barrett, "Write what I have spoken," and refrained from answering any questions. Later, he might listen to his recorded words in Apache, field questions, and "add information wherever he could be convinced that it was necessary" (xxi). Within a year the manuscript was completed and sent to President Roosevelt for his review. Roosevelt liked the story, calling it "a very interesting volume." He also advised Barrett to "disclaim responsibility in all cases where the reputation of an individual [was] assailed." Barrett followed Roosevelt's admonition, disavowing "responsibility for adverse criticisms of any persons mentioned by Geronimo" (xxiii).

In his "Preface," Barrett stated that he hoped the collaborative work would "give the reading public an authentic record of the private life of the Apache Indians" and allow Geronimo "to state the causes which impelled him in his

The Making of Geronimo's Story

Although Geronimo's story was filtered through his second cousin Asa Daklugie (on right) and school administrator S. M. Barrett (on left) before its publication, the story remains a revealing, early account of Apache culture. (*Geronimo's Story of His Life*, Taken Down and Edited by S. M. Barrett [New York: Duffield & Company, 1906], facing p. vi)

opposition to our civilization and laws" (v). The volume clearly achieved both goals. Divided into twenty-three chapters, *Geronimo's Story* opens with brief discussions of Apache cosmology, their early history, and tribal organization and institutions. Next follow two long parts on conflicts with "The Mexicans" and "The White Men." The final section treats Apache customs and religion and the later years of Geronimo, closing with a petition to President Roosevelt to allow the Apaches to return to their homelands in the Southwest.

The collaborative effort reveals a good deal about Apache sociocultural life and helps explain some of Geronimo's actions from the 1850s to the 1880s. Born in the 1820s, raised with a strong sense of place, tribal customs, and family allegiances, Geronimo became a warrior at seventeen and assumed the care of his widowed mother. Geronimo gloried in his warrior status: he "could go wherever [he] wanted and do whatever [he] liked." Soon thereafter he married and three children came into the family. He and his wife "followed the traditions of [their] fathers and were happy" (37, 39).

Then forces outside Geronimo's culture dramatically disrupted his idyllic life. These traumatic transformations, tensions, and conflicts led to tragedy. In the summer of 1858, Geronimo's tribe moved south across what Mexico and the United States considered a border but one without meaning to the Apache. There, while most of the men traded in an adjacent town, Mexican troops swooped down upon the Indians, killing the women and children in the camp, including Geronimo's mother, his wife, and his three children. These murders were the turning point in Geronimo's life. He had, he said, "lost all" (46). Thereafter Geronimo, following an acceptable Apache tradition, pursued eternal revenge against the Mexicans. Consumed with hatred, Geronimo raided year after year for nearly two decades in northern Mexico, attacking villages and traders, stealing and killing. Geronimo's animosity for Mexicans remained unabated as he talked to Barrett. "I have killed many Mexicans," he told the schoolman; "I do not know how many. . . . Some of them were not worth counting." Although Geronimo had not raided in Mexico for more than twenty years, he still considered Mexicans as "treacherous and malicious" (110). If he were young again, he would return to the warpath and go after his lifetime enemies in Old Mexico.

When Geronimo met his first Americans in about 1870, he was in his forties, a hardened warrior with a dozen years of guerilla conflict behind him. His attitudes toward "The White Men" changed, Geronimo tells us, when American soldiers both refused to keep their word and tried to kill off their Apache opponents. The soldiers, Geronimo insists, "never explained to the Government when an Indian was wronged, but always reported the misdeeds of the Indians. Much that was done by mean white men was reported at Washington as the deeds of my people." At this point, Barrett felt compelled to begin his disavowing footnotes: "This sweeping statement is more general than we are willing to concede, yet it may be more nearly true than our own accounts" (116).

As Geronimo's narrative makes clear, his people were increasingly caught between their Mexican opponents to the south and Americans invading from the north and east. From Geronimo's perspective, American soldiers were liars, except for General O. O. Howard. Of Howard Geronimo said: "he always kept his word with us and treated us as brothers. . . . We could have lived forever at peace with him" (128). The Apache leader is particularly critical of Generals George Crook and Nelson Miles, asserting that he left reservations on several occasions because these military leaders broke their word after nearly every agreement. Indeed, in one situation when an interpreter told Geronimo that "General Miles is your friend," Geronimo shot back: "I never saw him, but I have been in need of friends. Why has he not been with me" (172)?

The final chapters jumble discussions of Apache customs, Geronimo's changing ideas about religion, and his hopes for a better future. In contrasting the legal and social practices of warrior peoples with those of whites, Geronimo argues that Indian traditions are more equitable and accepting than American laws and the white men who have lied to him and treated him unjustly for twenty years. Geronimo details other sociocultural differences between Indians and his white captives that he discovered during his visits as onlooker, guest, and naif at several centennials and similar gatherings in the 1890s and early twentieth century. The chapter on religion contains parallel ambivalences. First, Geronimo describes Apache religious beliefs and then says: "Since my life as a prisoner has begun I have heard the teachings of the white man's religion, and in many respects believe it to be better than the religion of my fathers." He is not "ashamed to be a Christian," Geronimo adds; in fact, he has encouraged non-Christian Apaches "to study" Christianity "because it seems to me the best religion in enabling one to live right" (211–12). The final chapter asks President Roosevelt to review what's happened to Geronimo and his people, to see how treaty promises have been broken, and to return the Apache to their Arizona homelands. As captives they have to "wait until those in authority choose to act" (216).

What is one to make of this unusual narrative? Are its origins, composition, and authenticity too suspect, as some have argued, for it to be considered a useful document? What impact has the autobiography had on historians and novelists? What does its reception reveal about the nature of the western story and its solidification in the early years of the twentieth century?

Obviously, like most of the "told to" Native American autobiographies, *Geronimo's Story* is a complex cultural document. With no extant manuscript to consult, one cannot clearly sort out the roles of Geronimo, the interpreter Daklugie, and the editor Barrett in the formation of the book. Since Geronimo would not allow extensive transcription at the time of the interviews, how much of the collaborative interview belongs to Geronimo, how much to Barrett? A few of Barrett's intrusions seem evident, however. When the narrative speaks of a "primitive skirt" (24) Apache women wore and the tribe's "primitive worship" (207), the editor's jarring diction seems clear. Ironically, one scholar has argued that Barrett's unwillingness to take even more explicit stances in the narrative, introductory material, and endnotes undercuts the power of Geronimo's story.[42]

Despite these unanswered questions of composition and collaboration, Geronimo's autobiography remains a powerful counter narrative, a notable challenge to the traditional Wild West story. As Angie Debo, an authority on Geronimo, asserted seventy years later, the autobiography of Geronimo presented "the first account of the Apache wars from the inside out."[43] For the first time, historians, novelists, and film-makers had a credible story of the Opponents, of those peoples so often used as foils in tales of the Old West. Geronimo provided a holistic account; the unities of place, religion, warrior status, and tribal culture flow out from his narrative. True, Geronimo frequently casts himself as an "innocent victim," but in doing so he nonetheless furnishes the ethnographic and military detail missing in most pre–World War II stories of Indian-white conflict.

Consider, for example, a brief passage that occurs in Geronimo's account just before his final surrender. He dramatizes the dilemmas facing the Apache in these traumatic times:

> We were reckless of our lives, because we felt that every man's hand was against us. If we returned to the reservation we would be put in prison and killed; if we stayed in Mexico they would continue to send soldiers to fight us; so we gave no quarter to anyone and asked no favors. (141)

Nor should one overlook another succinct illustration of the holism among the Apache. Geronimo says tersely: "War is a solemn religious matter" (188). These and dozens of other observations from Geronimo furnish a perspective much at variance from contemporary accounts by and about such U.S. military leaders as Generals Custer, Crook, and Miles.

It is now evident that Geronimo's story had little impact on the next generation. Issued by an obscure New York publisher, not widely circulated, and unreviewed in leading historical and literary journals, the slim volume attracted scant notice. Leading western historians such as Frederick Jackson Turner and Frederic Logan Paxson seemed unaware of the book's existence. Nor did novelists adopt Geronimo's sympathetic view of the Apache before the late 1920s. Although anthropologists such as Morris E. Opler and Grenville Goodwin added probing, balanced studies of the Apache during the 1930s and early 1940s, not until after World War II did a new crop of novels, histories,

Geronimo's
Story of His Life

Taken Down and Edited by

S. M. BARRETT

Superintendent of Education, Lawton, Oklahoma

NEW YORK
DUFFIELD & COMPANY
1906

Geronimo's Story of His Life (1906)

S. M. Barrett's account of Geronimo, based on several conversations with the imprisoned Apache leader, illustrates the early "as told to" narratives about Native Americans.

and films present more positive images of the Apache. By the 1970s and 1980s, however, as C. L. Sonnichsen points out, so dramatic was the pendulum swing that Geronimo the Good had replaced Geronimo the Bad.[44]

Not surprisingly, then, Geronimo's story was not spliced into the Wild West story emerging in the early twentieth century. A society convinced that Indians must become agriculturists and become like white people, as the important Dawes Act of 1887 implied, was not inclined to celebrate the contestatory story of an "uncivilized" Indian. Although Geronimo helped preserve the previously unrecorded side of Indian-white conflicts, most custodians of culture were convinced that Indians were little more than innocent children in need of giant doses of civilizing. The less said about their nomadic and warrior days, the better for whites and Natives alike.[45]

FOR Mourning Dove (Christine Quintasket, Crystal McLeod, Mrs. Fred Galler) life may have been even more complex than for Geronimo. Of Colville and Okanogan heritage and an enrolled member of the Colville Tribe of north-central Washington, Mourning Dove longed to write a romance novel of the West. But she also wished to speak for her people and to show how they had been mistreated in the Far Corner of the United States and Canada. If those conflicting dreams often short-circuited her novelistic efforts, they nonetheless led to the eventual publication of *Cogewea, The Half-Blood: A Depiction of the Great Montana Cattle Range* (1927), perhaps the first novel by a Native American woman, and a milestone in the emergence of Indian voices in American literature.[46]

Mourning Dove was born in the 1880s in the narrow panhandle of Idaho. The daughter of Joseph Quintasket (Okanogan) and full-blood Lucy Stukin (Scho-yel-pi or Colville), she roamed with her family on both sides of the border from British Columbia to Alberta on the north and from Washington to Montana on the south. Her Indian name was Hum-ishu-ma (Mourning Dove), her name in English, Christine Quintasket. Adding to the complexities of her early years was her sporadic formal education. Her first attempts at schooling were particularly traumatic because teachers tried to force her to speak only in English when her home language was Salishan. In 1921 Mourning Dove listed schooling totaling ten years in four schools, but she always apologized for her semiliterate compositions.[47]

After her marriage to Hector McLeod (Flathead) in 1909, Mourning Dove

Mourning Dove (Christine Quintasket)

The youthful Native American Mourning Dove (Christine Quintasket) wanted to write a Western romance about the Montana open range. By its publication in 1927, however, *Cogewea* had been transformed into a much different kind of novel. (Courtesy Holland Library, Washington State University, Pullman, Washington)

and her husband labored as migrating field hands in the interior Pacific Northwest. Sadly, the union quickly disintegrated, and by 1912 she was in Portland trying to write her Western romance. Discouraged, thinking she could never turn out anything publishable, Christine (some of her letters are signed Crystal McLeod) put away the manuscript. She then enrolled in business college in Calgary, Alberta, hoping to improve her writing and typing skills. At about that time, she met Lucullus Virgil McWhorter at a Frontier Days celebration in Walla Walla, Washington. It was a friendship and literary collaboration that would mark the next two decades of her writing career.[48]

By the time the two met in 1914, Lucullus McWhorter was well into his career as a rancher, grassroots historian, and Indian rights advocate. Born in West Virginia in 1860 to an economically comfortable family, McWhorter demonstrated early on "a romantic and rebellious disposition." Still in the third grade at age twelve, he decided he had more to learn by roaming and reading, by reveling in the openness of the region's back country. Marrying and helping his father raise registered Devon cattle, he was bitten again with a restlessness to move west. Remarrying after the death of his first wife, McWhorter and his young family migrated to Ohio in 1897, where he continued to ranch. He also became increasingly involved in the study of frontier archaeology and history and even wrote a few frontier stories. A growing desire to be near Indians, a people who had fascinated him since boyhood, drove McWhorter to the Far West in 1903. Establishing a cattle ranch on the edge of Yakima, Washington, near the Yakima [now Yakama] Indian Reservation, he soon became acquainted with tribesmen and joined in their efforts to protect their reservation from greedy expansionists nearby. In 1913, he wrote *The Crime Against the Yakima,* a searing indictment of politicians and businessmen he considered the worst opponents of the Yakimas.

McWhorter was personally and emotionally deeply involved in issues involving Pacific Northwest Indians. In addition to his efforts on behalf of the Yakimas, he also served as a contractor and sponsor for Indians performing in regional roundups, rodeos, and festivals. While serving in this capacity, he and Mourning Dove first met in 1914 in Walla Walla. As one observer has noted, "Mourning Dove and McWhorter shared common ideological ground" when they first became acquainted.[49]

Within a few weeks of that meeting, McWhorter was encouraging Mourning Dove to complete her novel and to become involved in preserving the folklore and history of her people. During the winter of 1915–16, Mourning Dove came to stay with the McWhorters in Yakima while she and McWhorter re-vised and polished her drafted novel. They continued to work on the collab-oration, and by American entry into World War I they were attempting to market the novel. On at least two occasions McWhorter, serving as agent for the duo, thought he had the manuscript placed, but wartime paper shortages and other difficulties derailed publication efforts. Major surgery for McWhorter and the numbing death of his much-loved daughter brought fur-ther delays. During the 1920s, McWhorter continued to work on *Cogewea,* even as he became involved in a welter of other activities. In fact, as his biog-rapher points out, Big Foot (his adopted Indian name) too often took on more projects than he could handle, let alone finish. While contacting literary agents, writers, and well-known authors in the early 1920s to get their reactions to the manuscript and suggest possible revisions, McWhorter continued to revise and add to the novel. Then in 1925, the little-known Boston publisher The Four Seas Company offered to print the book if the collaborators would raise a substantial subsidy. Even after the subvention was raised, McWhorter had to threaten a suit before the book finally appeared in 1927.[50]

The plot of *Cogewea* is easily summarized. A young, attractive, and vivacious mixed-blood woman, Cogewea (little chipmunk) has returned from classes at the famed Carlisle Indian school to her sister and brother-in-law's ranch in western Montana. Although Cogewea participates in the ranch life and takes part in nearby social activities, she seems at loose ends until her traditional Grandmother Stemteema and eastern tenderfoot Alfred Densmore arrive to pull her in different directions. The grandmother chides Cogewea for not ad-hering to Native customs, and Densmore, thinking the mixed-blood young woman is wealthy, tries to woo her into marriage. Despite Stemteema's warn-ings and despite competition from the "breed" cowboy Jim, "Best Rider of the Flathead," the easterner persuades Cogewea to marry him. Once he learns that rumors of her wealth were a cowboy hoax, however, he abandons her, running off with one thousand dollars she has withdrawn for their honeymoon. After her initial shock and embarrassment, Cogewea recovers her liveliness, and two years later she and Jim marry in the final scene.

Even a cursory reading of *Cogewea* reveals it to be a deeply flawed work of fiction. Although the heroine often speaks for Indian culture and roundly crit-icizes white society, she much too easily succumbs to the evil man from the east. Her sudden decision to marry undercuts her credibility as a staunch de-fender of Native traditions and as a censurer of Euro-American society. More-

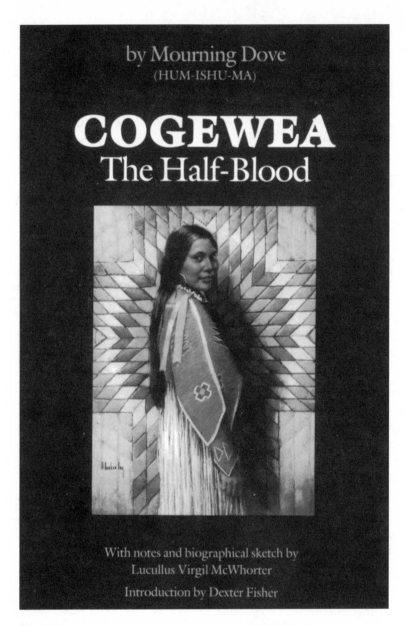

by Mourning Dove
(HUM-ISHU-MA)

COGEWEA
The Half-Blood

With notes and biographical sketch by
Lucullus Virgil McWhorter
Introduction by Dexter Fisher

Cogewea (1927)

   Cogewea (1927), one of the earliest novels coauthored by a Native American woman, is a revealing story about mixed bloods in the Pacific Northwest.

over, authorial intrusions say too much about Densmore's cupidity *before* his actions define that grasping nature. The grandmother figure provides important examples of Indian beliefs and customs, but beyond this important role as a keeper of tribal wisdom, she is not a fully rounded fictional character. Meanwhile, the jumble of cowpunchers furnish comic and emotional release from Cogewea's traumatic journey between Indian and white cultural pressures. They too, however, remain little more than stick figures, serving more as plot necessities than memorable characters.

As evident as these aesthetic sins are, they do not destroy the novel's significance as a cultural document. Nor do the literary flaws undercut Mourning Dove's importance as a silenced voice during the early twentieth century. Her perspective, if adopted, could have enriched the complexity and cultural significance of the western story in the early post-1900 period. From beginning to end, Mourning Dove's novel invokes allotment and assimilation pressures that Indians faced in the generation following the armed conflict and early reservation life that Geronimo experienced and related in his earlier story. In this way *Cogewea* illuminates additional traumas Native Americans faced in adjusting to postmilitary clashes and to a new generation on reservations.

Mourning Dove's book is structured around a series of sociocultural conflicts, ambiguities, and differences. The central tension is that between Indian and white ideas and actions. Stemteema, for example, speaks for an adherence to the moral, religious, courtship, and marriage customs of Native Americans. In contrast, the white villain Densmore epitomizes the dominating forces of East Coast civilization, power, and culture. Caught between these two systems, Cogewea, and to a lesser extent Jim and the other mixed-blood cowboys, suffers from "breed" backgrounds. These were ambiguities that Mourning Dove also experienced. On one occasion she wrote to McWhorter that she felt much more at home with half-breeds than with full-bloods, who "only laugh at me when I talk to them. So you savey, my position. It is h——to be a half breed."[51] Closely linked with these conflicts are differences between East and West. Densmore, civilization, education, and cultural power reside in the East, whereas Indians, cowboys, ranches, and small towns represent a less educated, less civilized, and less progressive West.

Several other conflicts power *Cogewea*. As the heroine attempts to find her way, men often stand as barriers. Densmore wants to dominate her, even her sympathetic brother-in-law is disappointed with what he considers her female wrongheadedness, and the cowboys, although admiring Cogewea, think she too often crosses into masculine territory. Other differences arise in the alternating chapters between Indian matters and the ranch hand activities. In trying to decide her future, the heroine finds herself caught between the "Indian" West and "cowboy or ranch" West. True, the occupational focus is that of the ranch. But that ranch, as something of a cultural flea market, hosts Indians, breeds, eastern dudes, and even a French cowboy. Finally, as an educated young woman, Cogewea wrestles with the "truth" of oral tradition and with the histories written by white historians.

In examining the meaning of these conflicts in this collaborative novel, one faces the major problem of voice and point of view. How much of the work belongs to Mourning Dove, how much to McWhorter? One scholar has succinctly defined the dilemma: "it is the complexity and extent of their collaboration that makes it so difficult to render a final evaluation of the novel."[52] Most recent interpreters stress, as they should, Mourning Dove's authorial presence. But that approach can be misleading. We know that Mourning Dove had completed a draft of *Cogewea* before she met her collaborator. We also know that she wanted to write a western romance that, while dealing with problems of contemporary Native Americans, would appeal to as wide an audience as possible. She hoped to write a best-seller.[53] McWhorter, on the other hand, wanted the work to be even less fictional, to be more authentic historically, and to be more pointed in its criticism of white society. Most of all, he wanted the novel to break from the yellowback, sensational western fiction he detested. He added the appended ethnographic notes, some of the poetic headnotes opening each chapter, and probably inserted most of the highly charged diatribes against whites and government agencies handling Indian affairs.[54] In fact, when Mourning Dove read the final published version, she wrote McWhorter, declaring she was "surprised at the changes you made. . . . I felt like it was some one elses book and not mine at all. In fact the finishing touches are put there by you, and I have never seen it. . . . Oh my Big Foot, you surely roasted the Shoapees [whites] strong. I think a little too strong to get their sympathy. I wish we had not gone too strong. . . . [*sic*]"[55] An unintended irony thus surfaced: Mourning Dove was probably less inclined than her Anglo-American collaborator to turn the novel into an attack on white society.

Despite its literary flaws and despite the unresolved questions about its authorship, *Cogewea* is a powerful illustration of dilemmas facing persons like

Mourning Dove. More than merely a novel of conflict between Indian and white, it is a story about connections, linkages, and marriages. Repeatedly, in the novel as well as in her private correspondence, Mourning Dove speaks of the traumas facing mixed breeds, those who are products of the mingling of two races. Cogewea, Jim, Cogewea's two sisters, and several of the cowboys wrestle with these hybrid identities. Will they remain Indian, will they take up white ways, or will they attempt assimilation of the two races? One emphasis, and surely this must have come from Mourning Dove rather than from McWhorter, suggests that accommodation cannot occur until white men stop betraying their Indian mates.[56] In the stories of Stemteema, in the lives of Cogewea and Jim, and in Mourning Dove's autobiography, white men's betrayal of their Indian wives leads to a variety of insecurities, breakdowns, and tragedies. Mourning Dove felt this betrayal powerfully and worked it into nearly all the major strains of her novel.

Unfortunately, the heroine of *Cogewea* and the cultural complexities she and her creator faced never found their way into the western narrative in the first decades of the twentieth century. Although novelists, film-makers, and biographers often used conflicts between Indians and whites as central emphases in their works, mixed bloods rarely became major characters. These omissions meant that stories about Indians and the "half-breed" as heroes were usually omitted in chronicles of the American West. Just as Geronimo's warrior tales were elided, so were the narratives of mixed bloods and Indians confronting pressures of assimilation. Those subjects would not be recovered and utilized until well after World War II.

Chapter Three

Traditional Stories

A FEW WEEKS after Owen Wister's *The Virginian* appeared to widespread acclaim, he wrote to his mother to answer her earlier criticisms of the novel. In parrying the opinionated, even imperial reactions of Sarah Butler Wister, her son not only defended the content, structure, and purposes of his notable work, he demonstrated how much his novel owed to stories written about the West since the Civil War. More revealing, and yet unknown to Wister, was the adumbrative quality of the novel. What Frederick Jackson Turner's essays were to frontier historians, what Frederic Remington and Charlie Russell were to later artists, and what Broncho Billy, William S. Hart, and Tom Mix were to cinematic storytellers, Wister's novel was to later western novelists.

In discussing *The Virginian* with his mother, Wister defended several of its major ingredients. He thought she was mistaken, for example, in labeling the novel "piecemeal" and in pointing to the "doubtful morality" of "the hero's conduct." Nor could he accept her criticism of the lynching scene or the superfluousness of the final chapter. He had to admit, however, that the heroine was a "failure"; she seemed "without personality" to Wister.[1] In defending the integrity of his novel's plot, his handling of the hero, and his use of conflict and violence, even while acknowledging the heroine's limitations, Wister tried to explain and maintain the strengths of his story before one of his most demanding critics. In these defenses he also aids later students in understanding how his pathbreaking novel helped to solidify the western story.

Within a few weeks after the publication of *The Virginian* on May 30, 1902, the novel rocketed to the top of the best-seller list, where it remained throughout 1902 and into 1903. In the first three months after publication, Wister's blockbuster sold more than 100,000 copies, and by the end of the year several reviewers were hailing it as the best novel of the year and the premier literary interpretation of the American West.[2]

Readers were particularly drawn to Wister's cowboy protagonist. The nameless hero of Wister's novel, while following in the footsteps of earlier frontier heroes, also opened the trail for hundreds of sagebrush horsemen who followed after him. Duplicating the courage of intrepid men like Daniel Boone and Kit Carson, Wister's cowpuncher also resembles James Fenimore Cooper's Leatherstocking in his willingness to confront dangerous foes and dutifully carry out difficult tasks assigned him. Similarly, his valiant actions and competitive drive parallel the heroes of Buffalo Bill's Wild West, and his romantic role in the novel follows the plot lines of dozens of dime novel Westerns. Those acquainted with earlier depictions of frontier heroes recognized how much Wister's hero owed to these previous western protagonists.

From the opening of *The Virginian,* Wister wanted his hero to be seen as a man apart. In the first chapter, in one of the most evocative paragraphs of the novel, the greenhorn narrator falls in love at first sight:

> Lounging there at ease against the wall was a slim young giant, more beautiful than pictures. His broad, soft hat was pushed back; a loose-knotted, dull-scarlet handkerchief sagged from his throat; and one casual thumb was hooked in the cartridge-belt that slanted across his hips. He had plainly come many miles from somewhere across the vast horizon, as the dust upon him showed. . . . But no dinginess of travel or shabbiness of attire could tarnish the splendor that radiated from his youth and strength. . . . Had I been the bride, I should have taken the giant, dust and all.[3]

In his physical appearance, in his ability to handle his opponents, in the strength that radiates from his movements, Wister's hero is nature's nobleman. On another occasion, upset with the Wyoming rancher Balaam's vicious mistreatment of horses, the Virginian swings into action with the speed and muscle of an unleashed superman. "Vengeance like a blast struck Balaam," Wister writes. "The Virginian hurled him to the ground, lifted and hurled him again, lifted him and beat his face and struck his jaw. . . . [Balaam] fended his eyes as best he could against these sledge-hammer blows of justice" (310).

In addition to exhibiting the physical powers of the Anglo heroes of the frontier, the Virginian is a "man [who] knows his business" (3). A superb horseman who understands animals and people, he's also wise in the ways of handling men. He cavorts with his cowpuncher friends, pleases his boss the Judge

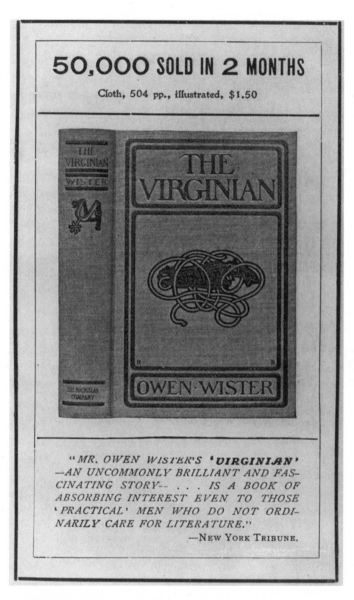

The Virginian (1902)

More than any other novel, *The Virginian* (1902), by Owen Wister, synthesized the major ingredients of the western story early in the twentieth century. (Courtesy Owen Wister Papers, Manuscript Division, Library of Congress, Washington, D.C.)

in handling a remuda of revolting cowboys, and finally curbs and carts off the treasonous badman Trampas. In the words of one critic, the Virginian is a model for later fictional heroes because of his "superior perception," his "ability to see *through* appearances to the real meanings of things." This "superiority of insight" allows the hero to be above and beyond his masculine competitors and even to perceive truths in Shakespeare and in other writers that startle his more educated and more widely read acquaintances.[4]

Through his palpable, clear strengths, the hero serves as lawbringer and civilizer. Although depicted as a law-abiding man who upholds society's institutions, the hero, when necessity arises, can move outside the law like earlier dime novel worthies who broke the law to protect it. The Virginian also participates in illegal vigilante actions to quell a rustler gang, even though it means helping to string up his former saddlemate Steve. In that series of traumatic events and in his shootdown with Trampas on the main street of Medicine Bow in the novel's penultimate chapter, the Virginian defends his actions against charges of illegality—even murder. He asks the heroine Molly Wood the day before their wedding, when he tries to explain his need to face down the villain Trampas, "Can't yu' see how it must be about a man" (478)? Before he can marry, before he can take his place in the nascent society as a husband, he must defend his honor. This emotional request for the woman to understand what the hero must do reverberates through later Westerns, from John Wayne's "A man's gotta do what a man's gotta do" to other declarations of heroes' needs to prove their courage and masculinity in the face of villainous challenges and emotional feminine denunciations of violence. Acting out Wister's own beliefs, the Virginian moves outside the law so that, in the long run, he can help save it for civilization.

In still another way, Wister's hero served as a model for hundreds of later fictional and cinematic protagonists. Without aristocratic backgrounds, minus a distinguished family, and lacking an education, the Virginian nonetheless proves himself a man among men. In outsmarting the evil Trampas, in proving his worth to the Judge, and in demonstrating his grassroots horse sense, he acts out the narrator's declaration that "true democracy" in the United States is allowing "the best man [to] win." When that happens, "true democracy and true aristocracy are one and the same thing" (147). In equating true quality and equality, Wister was, as he wrote in a new "Preface" to a reprinting of his novel in 1911, telling an "American story," providing "an expression of American faith." In this expansive metaphorical calculus, Wister's cowpuncher, in gallantly standing against and defeating his enemies, epitomized larger ordeals. He represented all Americans in "the test of Democracy"; like the Virginian, they too must withstand the threats to the American way of life in the early twentieth century.⁵ By investing the hero of his influential and successful story with such large symbolical significance, Wister provided an irresistible character who, in exact or revised form, inhabited thousands of Westerns in the first half of the twentieth century.

If Wister's handling of his hero clearly built on and expanded the protagonists of Cooper, Cody's Wild West, and dozens of dime novels, he parted company with these precedents for his villains in *The Virginian*. In his novel—in fact in nearly all of his writing—Wister did little with Indians. He knew little about Native Americans. By the time he arrived in the northern West and the Southwest, most Indians had been defeated and shoved on to reservations. In *The Virginian,* a group of Indians illegally off a reservation severely wound the Virginian, but neither this nor any other band of Native Americans is the chief villain of any of Wister's book-length western fiction. Indians as primary opponents, so much in evidence in Cooper's fiction, the dime novels, and Buffalo Bill's extravaganzas, are nearly a disappearing race in Wister's longer works. Revealingly, the same was true for many western novels in the decades immediately following 1900.

Wister turned to other character types for his antagonists in *The Virginian*. These "bad guys" provide clear illustrations of Wister's beliefs about the molding power of the West and his social philosophy. Much attracted to the West's novel landscapes during his first trips to the region in the late 1880s and early 1890s, Wister gradually became convinced that the West could also misshape those unable to withstand its stern demands. On one occasion, after watching a rancher gouge out the eye of a horse (an incident used in *The Virginian* to depict Balaam, the maltreater of horses), Wister wrote in his western journals: "I begin to conclude from five seasons of observation that life in this negligent irresponsible wilderness tends to turn people shiftless, cruel, and incompetent."⁶ All of the villains (save the Indians) in Wister's novel—Trampas, Steve, Balaam, and the pathetic Shorty—cannot satisfactorily find their ways in this wilderness West. Trampas, Steve, and Shorty become rustlers and eventually lose their lives because of their extralegal actions. Steve, the Virginian's friend, falls before easy money; he is "disturbed over getting rich quick and being a big man in the Territory" (399). Shorty is even less able to stand up to the demands of the West. As the hero tells the narrator, "Now back East you can be middling and get along. But if you go to try a thing on in this Western country, you've got to do it *well*. You've got to deal cyards *well;* you've got to steal *well*. . . . You must break all the Commandments *well* in this Western country. . . ." (401–2).

Trampas represents the heart of villainy. He helps lead Steve and Shorty astray; he calls the hero a son of a bitch and insults the heroine. Trampas also challenges the Virginian's masculinity and courage in the resonant SOB scene, he tests the hero's leadership in the frog escapade, and finally he shoots first in their standoff at sundown. Most of all, however, he tries to subvert the society that the hero repeatedly supports. Trampas contests against the institutions that, if supported, will bring what the hero (and quite probably Wister) considers civilization and community to a Wild West. The evil-hearted villain undermines the value of women and marriage, he undercuts ownership of property, and he continually defies persons who try to close out a wild frontier. Quite simply, in attempting to disrupt or destroy the good society that the hero, the heroine, and the ranchers and townspeople are trying to establish and maintain, Trampas epitomizes moral and social disorder and is assigned a black hat for his efforts. His antisocial progeny inhabit thousands of fictional and cinematic Westerns.

The other notable male figure in the novel is the greenhorn easterner, the "I" narrator through whose consciousness much of the story is told. His central role deserves more attention. By utilizing this naive narrator (another more omniscent storyteller also narrates part of the story) Wister doubles his story line: parallel to the Virginian's lessons on responsibility, leadership, and marriage, the "I" storyteller learns equally traumatic parables about the frontier West, the nature of equality, and the code of the cowboy country. Moreover, since the greenhorn obviously represents eastern ways, his clashes with frontier social customs provide an East-West confrontation that Wister took great pains to portray.[7]

The narrator quickly learns of his outsider status, but he's slow to change his alienating behaviour. When he assumes an unwarranted familiarity with the Virginian, the hero speaks of the "right smart . . . oddities . . . [that] come in on every train." After a few moments of a self-refection, the narrator realizes he can "not be jocular" with the cowpuncher. "This handsome, ungrammatical son of the soil had set between us the bar of his cold and perfect civility" (10, 11). Gradually, he learns to keep his mouth shut, to follow in conversations rather than to open them, to listen to the words and stories of experienced westerners. Watching the Virginian and learning from those actions, the narrator experiences moments of epiphany that help him understand himself and this strange, new West. Although often "styled" the "tenderfoot" (67), he learns important new lessons. When the hero outsmarts Trampas and heads off a threatened cowboy rebellion, for example, the narrator proves he's no longer a total greenhorn, sensing, as he says, that the Virginian's courage and wiles have "been equal to the occasion: that is the only kind of equality which I recognize" (202).

In the second half of the novel the narrator becomes a different kind of person. Now he comes at the Virginian's bidding to eastern Idaho, as the hero faces the most wrenching event of his life. Beginning his journey to find the Virginian in the Saw Tooth Range in interior Idaho, the narrator recalls his "Eastern helplessness in the year when we had met first." Now, he adds, "I enjoyed thinking how I had come to be trusted . . . . Now I was crossing unmapped spaces with no guidance. The man who could do this was scarce any longer a 'tenderfoot'" (379). When the Virginian confronts the emotional chaos following his participation in the vigilante hanging of Steve, his friend turned rustler, he relies on the maturing narrator as his confidant. As literary critic John Seelye discerningly notes, when the Virginian and the former greenhorn camp along Superstition Trail and the hero blubbers out his emotional loss and guilt, he does so to an equal.[8] If this male camaraderie in the far-western wilderness lacks the racial implications of earlier male bondings in Cooper's Leatherstocking Tales, Herman Melville's *Moby Dick,* and Mark Twain's *Huckleberry Finn,* it does resonate with regional and class meanings, by uniting a polished easterner with a southern farm boy turned western cowboy.

The power and persuasiveness of Wister's narrator figure derive from two major sources. Much of the narrator's story clearly parallels Wister's experiences. His western journals reveal how much his coming of age echoed that of the narrator. For both, the rite of passage from eastern stuffiness to friendship and acceptance among western cowpunchers is cast in the form of a *bildungsroman*. Wister too could identify with the narrator in his story of emergence. The storyteller says of his new relationship with the Virginian that they "were thorough friends," "all other barriers between" them now gone. Wister also realized that he could tell his story more movingly if a narrator, while undergoing his own ordeals, could serve as a chorus in commenting on the Virginian's journey to maturity, responsibility, and marriage. Through the narrator, Wister provided both intimacy with and distance from the main character.

Owen Wister

Owen Wister first came west in 1885. By the late 1890s he was well
known for his stories and novels about cowboys, Indians, and frontier
soldiers. (Courtesy of the American Heritage Center, University of
Wyoming, Laramie, Wyoming)

Unfortunately, nearly all this attraction and power are missing in Wister's ineffectual portrait of Molly Wood, the novel's heroine. Granted, Wister had few fictional models to follow in creating strong female characters. Most heroines of nineteenth-century American male authors were an anemic sort, although Nathaniel Hawthorne's Hester Prynne remains a notable exception. Nor had Cooper, Buffalo Bill's Wild West, dime novel Westerns, or Local Color writers like Bret Harte, Alfred Henry Lewis, or Joaquin Miller created memorable heroines. In the short stories and novels of Mary Hallock Foote, which Wister knew and appreciated, he had usable models, but Wister, like most other writers telling the western story before the 1960s, preferred to tell a man's story. As a result, in *The Virginian,* as in most of Wister's other writings, his female characters usually play supporting or catalytic rather than central roles.[9]

In trying to create a believable heroine in Molly Wood, Wister shared a major problem with other writers treating the West. In the public's eye the frontier story represented masculine courage and individualism in fronting demanding landscapes and human competitors. Contemporary gender expectations meant that women could rarely act in the protagonist's role; instead, they might initially compete or contest with the hero, but they usually ended up agreeing with, often marrying, him. At first, Molly Wood spars with the Virginian and even plans to leave Wyoming to move back to New England. But after his wounding and during her stint of nursing him back to health, she gradually succumbs to his declarations of love. Later, as they ride to Medicine Bow to exchange their vows, Molly realized that "by love and her surrender to him their positions had been exchanged. He was not now, as through his long courting he had been, her half-obeying, half-refractory worshiper. She was no longer his half-indulgent, half-scornful superior" (450–51). In a final act of independence, she tells him she will not marry him if he takes on Trampas in a duel to death. But when he survives that terrible competition and returns to the hotel, Molly, breathing out "Oh, thank God" (485), falls into his arms.[10]

In adding a love story between the leading man and woman, Wister grafted a new ingredient onto the western story that subsequent writers of Westerns rarely omitted. Although Cooper's Leatherstocking hero suffered several pangs of heart, he never married. Dime novels frequently featured a romance between the hero and heroine or between another man and woman in a subplot, and even some of Wister's previous stories contained prominent love stories. But none of these works blended as attractively and as successfully as *The Virginian* a Wild West moving toward civilization, a handsome and courageous cowboy hero, and a heart-warming romance with a perky and pretty schoolmarm. Quite possibly Molly Wood lacks depth because her individual identity is sacrificed to the author's plot demands. In Wister's fictional blueprint, Molly serves in an important but subservient position, furnishing the love interest for the dashing hero and representing an eastern genteel culture, but she does not exist as a strong, individualistic figure in her own right.

Finally, Wister infused his story with a romantic, nostalgic mood by telling a yarn about a much-cherished vanishing frontier. In a prefatory section addressed "To the Reader," Wister noted that wild Wyoming from 1874 and 1890, a territory replete with "primitive joys and dangers," had now passed from the scene. Actually, Wister had been writing of a disappearing frontier for at least a decade. In delineating vanishing cowboys, he wrote in one short story published in 1892: "They gallop over the face of the empty earth for a little while, and those whom rheumatism or gunpowder does not overtake, are blotted out by the course of empire, leaving no trace behind." Three years later in his classic essay, "The Evolution of the Cow-Puncher," written at the request of artist Frederic Remington, Wister chronicled the rise, flowering, and decline of the cowboy. "Now departed, never to return . . . except where he lingers in the mountains of New Mexico," the cowpuncher, Wister wrote, was the descendant of a rich, worthy Anglo-Saxon strain. But now Progress has driven them from the field. We are left, as Wister said of Remington's painting *The Last Cavalier,* which illustrated Wister's essay, to "withdraw and mourn" for a Past that "will haunt [us] forever."[11]

This elegiac tone characterizes much of *The Virginian*. Like his contemporaries, historian Frederick Jackson Turner and artists Remington and Charlie Russell, Wister loved the older frontier and ambivalently faced the changes his novel records. Although the greenhorn narrator reacts to the open landscape like a schoolboy on the first day of vacation, he quickly sees evidence of a vanishing frontier. Traveling salesmen already peddle their wares in Medicine Bow, and canned goods play "a great part in the opening of [the] new country." In fact, "these picnic pots and cans were the first of her trophies that Civilization dropped upon Wyoming's virgin soil. The cowboy is now gone to worlds invisible . . . but the empty sardine box lies rusting over the face of the Western earth" (43). Later in the novel, the appearance of women, resulting marriages, a crop of offspring, and a new school "symbolized the dawn of a neighborhood, and [they] brought a change into the wilderness air. The feel of [them] struck cold upon the free spirits of the cow-punchers, and they told each other that, what with women and children and wire fences, this country would not long be a country for men" (97).

In the closing chapters, the conflict intensifies between an open, free, and unfettered frontier and a cultivated, institution-driven West. Even as the Virginian and his bride-to-be ride toward town, marriage, and an unexpected showdown with Trampas, his heart is in the mountains, where they will honeymoon. "The free road," which they travel, "became wholly imprisoned, running between unbroken stretches of barbed wire" (461). At the end of that fenced-in road await the violent guns of Trampas. But after Evil falls before Good, the Virginian and Molly escape to their high meadow Eden. There, in the "true world," which "belonged to no man, for it was deep in the unsurveyed and virgin wilderness" (486, 487), they will drink in the peace, purity, and seclusion of their beloved bower. While there, the Virginian confesses to his new wife that even though he will be a responsible husband, he longs to retain the freedom of the wild animal they see in the woods.

This oxymoronic yoking of the wild and civilized continues to the end of *The Virginian*. When the newly marrieds visit Molly's relatives in New England, the hero strikes them as a handsome cowboy dressed in "homespun suit" but whose conversation "seemed fit to come inside the house" (501). And when Molly's maiden aunt speaks of the West, the Virginian tells her it's changing rapidly. Although the Cattle King West is still "having its day," he adds "we are getting ready for the change—some of us are" (504). On the final page, the Virginian has become a ranch partner, bought land with coal deposits, and begun a family; but, simultaneously, the older times are longed for, and his oldest son still rides the horse that the hero loved during his bachelor days.

Wister's notable novel fixed the West as a closing frontier in the minds of the American reading public. Most writers of the previous century portrayed the West as a beckoning frontier in which explorers, travelers, and migrants faced awesome landscapes and new peoples that challenged and often redirected their minds and hearts. Wister represented a fresh generation of writers forced to wrestle with a frontierless America. More than any other early twentieth-century novel, *The Virginian* represented a break from nineteenth-century stories of an open, expanded frontier; it carried instead a new, alarming message that the magic frontier had disappeared over the horizon.

In retrospect, *The Virginian* proved to be a watershed moment in the development of the western story. Drawing upon earlier frontier narratives and adding new ingredients, Wister produced the metastory of the frontier. Synthesizing these diverse strains, Wister's blockbuster novel defined the Western: the story of a white male's adventures on the frontier undergoing ordeals of competition with alien landscapes. To these earlier components, Wister added a strain of romance, a greenhorn narrator, romantic descriptions of the cowboy as the archetypal frontier hero, and furnished a nostalgic rendering of a closing frontier. Solidified and endlessly repeated, these ingredients became the most widely recognized elements of the western story until the 1960s.

THE Old West was born again in the 1920s. Like the closing decades of the nineteenth century and the later 1950s, the decade and a half following World War I seemed aflame with interest in a Wild West. This fascination burned across nearly every facet of American cultural life. Zane Grey's yearly fictional Westerns topped best-seller lists in the 1920s, and in the same decade cinematic Westerns, by far, were the most popular movie genre. In the same years, frontier histories by Frederick Jackson Turner and Frederic Logan Paxson won major acclaim, and hundreds of thousands of Americans flocked west to rough it easy on Dude Ranches sprouting all over the West.

At the same time a gathering remuda of journalist-historians churned out more than two dozen book-length biographies of lively western heroes and heroines. Less well known than the novels, movies, and prize-winning histories of the twenties, these appealingly written biographies were part and parcel of the Old West story as it gradually solidified in the first decades of the twentieth century. Buffalo Bill Cody, Wyatt Earp, Wild Bill Hickok, Calamity Jane, and Billy the Kid—all these Wild West demigods were subject to at least one biography in the decade stretching from the mid-twenties to the mid-thirties. Nearly all the biographies came from journalists; nearly all these writers wrote positive or at least sympathetic portraits of their subjects and of the closing frontier they depicted.

The most significant of these journalist-historians was Walter Noble Burns. His best-selling *Saga of Billy the Kid* did more than any of the other biographies to influence the Wild West histories that appeared during the interwar years.[12] A Chicago newspaperman since the turn of the century, Burns had written on a variety of historical, biographical, and literary subjects, including Wild Bill Hickok, before he came to New Mexico in 1923 to research a story of Billy the Kid. An indefatigable researcher, an ambitious interviewer, and a stunning storyteller, Burns crisscrossed the state for three months, taking oral histories from most of the major survivors of New Mexico's Lincoln County War of the late 1870s. He also skimmed newspaper accounts of the 1870s and 1880s and read some of the previous accounts of Billy and the war. But other available sources he did not use. He was unable to obtain a copy of Pat Garrett's *The Authentic Life of Billy the Kid, Noted Desperado of the Southwest,* published in 1882, a year after Billy's death, and Burns dismissed the other early book on the Kid, Charlie Siringo's *History of 'Billy the Kid'* (1920), as a weak, ineffective piece of work.[13]

Writing at a fast pace after completing his research and while he continued his newspaper job in Chicago, Burns quickly finished his manuscript. *The Saga of Billy the Kid* appeared in the Spring of 1926 to universal acclaim. Selected as one of the first choices of the new Book of the Month Club, the dramatic biography and history made Burns overnight a good deal of money and a well-known writer. Even before 1930, the *Saga* generated more than twenty-five thousand dollars in royalties and helped lead to the quick publication of Burns's two later books on the Old West: *Tombstone: An Iliad of the Southwest* (1927) and *The Robin Hood of El Dorado: The Saga of Joaquin Murrieta, Famous Outlaw of California's Age of Gold* (1932). Before his premature death in 1932, Burns was often mentioned as a major interpreter of the nineteenth-century frontier.[14] In addition, although infrequently mentioned, Walter Noble Burns furnished a story line for biographers and historians in spinning new narratives of the West, even as he built on stories already in circulation about the Old West.

A few weeks after the publication of the *Saga,* a journalist interviewed Burns, asking him "what book he would rather have written than any other." His response to the question and his comments about the overlap between history and fiction reveal much about Burns's goals in writing his book on Billy the Kid and the Lincoln County War. Telling the interviewer that he was "essentially a reporter" and that facts were "the biggest things in the world" for him, and that therefore his "literary leaning" was "toward fact books-history, biography," Burns nonetheless argued that "history at its best" was "a drama of facts." So he wished that he had written Thomas Carlyle's *French Revolution,* a gigantic book that made the facts of the past "live with the warmth and color of their immediate day." Then, in capsule phrases Burns summarized what he thought of Carlyle: his appeal was "his marvelous ability to visualize the past, to interpret a situation or a personality in the quick beauty of a phrase, to re-

The Saga of Billy
▼ the Kid ▼

BY WALTER NOBLE BURNS
Author of "A Year With A Whaler"

▼▼   ▼▼

▼▼   ▼▼

GARDEN CITY   NEW YORK
DOUBLEDAY, PAGE & COMPANY
1926

The Saga of Billy the Kid (1926)

   The Saga of Billy the Kid (1926), written by journalist Walter Noble Burns, exemplifies the numerous histories published in the interwar years lionizing major Wild West figures.

produce with vital clarity all the physical and spiritual drama of a picturesque and tremendous epoch."[15] Put differently, good writing must capture the drama and color of history, else it became the boring details of a dead past. This artistic credo shaped the content of Burns's Billy. Ironically, even as this artistic design pleased storytelling biographers, historians, and general readers, it became a bone of contention for fact-minded chroniclers, then and later.

From the opening pages of *Saga,* Burns makes clear his intention to tell a dramatic story. Invoking comparisons with ancient heroes and battles, Burns locks his characters in a titanic conflict for the control of New Mexico. The first two chapters pit John Chisum ("The King of the Valley") against L. G. Murphy ("The Lord of the Mountains") as the author creates the first of a string of stirring battles that drive his narrative. Nothing moves slowly or smoothly in the *Saga;* one sequence of squabbles leads pell-mell into the next. Once the two groups of partisans fire off their first shots and reach an emotional pitch in a three-[five]-day battle in the town of Lincoln in mid-July 1878, Burns quickly creates other intense conflicts that continue until Pat Garrett guns down Billy three years later in old Ft. Sumner. No contemporary reviewer or reader complained that Burns's book lacked verve or vivacity. In fact, one amateur historian spoke for many others when he said the story exuded lively writing; the *Saga* kept him up nearly all night with its engrossing plot.[16]

Revealingly, the same storytelling techniques alienated other readers. Indeed, some complained that Burns obviously sacrificed authenticity to sensationalism. Still others claimed that Burns blatantly took sides in the civil war, that he fell captive to those persons he interviewed, and that too often he was clearly mistaken. There was some basis for these criticisms. In locking his many characters into a sequence of clashes, Burns stressed differences and frequently underestimated the intraparty squabbles that divided the Chisum-John Tunstall-Alex McSween-Billy faction on one side and "The House" cabal of Murphy, J. J. Dolan, the Santa Fe Ring, and the military on the other. Similarly, Burns's extensive interviews with Sallie Chisum Robert, Paulita Maxwell Jaramillo, Susan McSween Barber, and Ighenio [Yginio] Salazar predisposed him to side with opponents of the House. Early on Burns tipped his hand when he wrote: "it is now clear that Murphy's cause was basically wrong and McSween's basically right; that Murphy was an unscrupulous dictator, McSween the champion of principle; that Murphy stood for lawlessness, McSween for law" (50). In nearly every subsequent chapter Burns paired opponents, often in such uneven comparisons.

Burns's controversial description of the tense final hours in the McSweens' burning home at the climax of the Lincoln County War engendered the harshest criticism of his work. Most of these dramatic pages drew heavily on Susan McSween's memories forty-five years later, but Burns also added events and descriptions that Susan furiously denounced. When she read an earlier essay summarizing the *Saga* and a year later the full account, she erupted in anger at Burns's depiction of her playing the *Star Spangled Banner* on her piano as her home burned. Meanwhile, Burns depicted Susan's husband Alex, a devoutly religious man, as cowering in the corner with a bible in his hand and then stumbling through the burning kitchen door into the backyard where he fell before a blizzard of enemy bullets.

Not surprisingly, Susan denounced these portrayals as "ridiculous" and untrue. What had she cared, she told another historian, "about a piano in comparison to our lives." The description of her playing the *Star Spangled Banner* was "the biggest lie [there] ever was," she added.[17] But when Susan wrote directly to Burns, she followed a different line, telling him she had "never condemned the book." His work, she continued, was "well written and very interesting and the whole US is interested in it. You have made me famous and I thank you for the god [*sic*] things you said of me." Still, she wondered why Burns had pictured her as playing the piano during those traumatic times. Susan was "hurt" because she thought readers would think her a "daring course [*sic*] roundish woman." Moreover, she continued, her husband may have been a Christian but not the "fool" he seemed to be in Burns's account. She hoped now that someone, perhaps her friend Maurice Garland Fulton, would write the full, true story of the troubling times in New Mexico she had survived.[18]

Even more revealing are the reactions of Burns to these criticisms. At first, Burns told Professor Fulton that he had carefully researched his book; he had "an authority for every statement [he] had made." "You are wrong," he also told Fulton, "in assuming that my attitude is that of fiction writer." Rather, Burns was both a "serious seeker after information of historical accuracy" and interested in the "drama" of his story. He knew of "no story of the Old West . . . so full of dramatic interest." Less than a month after Burns's *Saga* appeared, he sent Susan McSween Barber a copy, telling her he had tried to make her "the heroine." Readers, he was convinced, would "have the very finest opinion of [her] character, courage and heroism." And in a phrase that must have touched her vanity, Burns told Susan that he had "made [her] fame permanent between the covers of a book." With Alex McSween, Burns had faced a different dilemma. He had wondered how to treat Susan's husband, finally deciding he would portray the Lincoln lawyer "as a religious enthusiast who died a martyr to his religious convictions and principles." McSween, quite deliberately, was "dramatized," going to "his death devoid of fear and with his thoughts fixed on spiritual things."[19]

Then, Burns mentioned the event that had upset Susan the most. "The incident of your playing 'The Star Spangled Banner,'" he wrote, "was told me in New Mexico by a number of people. It is a part of the legend and it is so dramatic and so heroic, in my opinion, that it would not do to throw it out." Three years later, Burns confessed to a businessman well acquainted with the history of Billy and the Lincoln County War that in the *Saga* "he put the bible in McSween's hands [and] that Mrs. McSween never played the Star Spangled Banner on the piano." By this time, Burns admitted to the inaccuracies of his account and hoped that he might prepare a revised edition that corrected the mistakes.[20]

More significant in the larger picture of Walter Noble Burns as a western storyteller is his memorable portrait of a Wild West. Undoubtedly, Burns attracted many appreciative readers through his portrayal of New Mexico as a lawless, violent, and romantic faraway frontier. His West is a magic land, bubbling with battles between larger-than-life protagonists and villains. Lincoln, New Mexico, Burns wrote, "was hard-boiled from the first" (31). On those "boundless, fenceless plains" (36), a "bloody vendetta" took place that included "hard-eyed men standing in sinister groups in the street" of Lincoln (45). In Burns's view, southeastern New Mexico, with its Lincoln County War, was a "culture-bed of many kinds and degrees of desperadoes" (56). When Billy the Kid and a group like him ride out, ostensibly as a posse in pursuit of the murderers of John Tunstall, Burns describes them as "bold fellows" but also as a remuda of "desperate and lawless men" (85).

As Buffalo Bill and the dime novelists had in the nineteenth century and as Wister did in *The Virginian*, Burns painted the West as a wild, uncivilized arena in which to test his stalwart characters. As we've seen, the cattle baron John Chisum built and maintained his sprawling domain through his shrewd, unrelenting drive. John Tunstall and Alex McSween, on the other hand, succumb to the relentless demands of this wild place and the vicious men who oppose him. Even the newcomer and political appointee Lew Wallace gives up on the savage Southwest. Meanwhile, Burns saves a special role for Pat Garrett in the second half of the *Saga*.

Burns carefully constructs a chaotic frontier pitting two groups in a "bloody vendetta" before he brings his central figure Billy the Kid on the scene. Then, briefly and deftly, the author limns the character of the young protagonist, not so much as a hero as the lead figure of the story. Billy is described as the marriage of opposites, "knightly devotion . . . [accentuated] with a spirit of primitive savagery." Billy had become, like earlier demigods such as Robin Hood, Claude Duval, and Dick Turpin, a "symbol of frontier-errantry, a figure of eternal youth riding forever through a purple glamour of romance" (52, 53). Fate, boyish enthusiasm, tragedy, incessant battles, a vendetta, and an ever-present smile—these experiences formed and described Billy the Kid. Burns, in a mini-psychobiography of the Kid, describes him as a split personality, a youth with a "desperado complex" (55). Unlike Wild Bill Hickok, whom Burns pictures as a "good 'bad man'" "killing many men to establish peace," Billy lived in "the most murderous spot of the West." In that place, he became "a genius painting his name in flaming colours with a six-shooter across the sky of the Southwest" (55–56).

Even while Burns presents a series of appealing word pictures depicting conflict after conflict, Billy more and more emerges as the offspring of the older, lawless West. Settling his clashes with his blazing guns, living from his rustling, and choosing not to marry and settle down, Billy the Kid epitomizes one side of what historian Richard Maxwell Brown calls the "Western Civil War of Incorporation."[21] Early on, Billy seems the young Robin Hood fighting against the monopolistic Murphy-Dolan contingent and their territorial cousins, the Santa Fe Ring; but once Tunstall and McSween are murdered and John Chisum withdraws in early 1878 from the escalating war, Billy gradually assumes leadership of the House opponents. As the unacknowledged leader of "The Regulators," Billy is ironically portrayed as an anachronistic throwback, refusing to recognize the power of incoming law and order. In the closing chapters, Billy emerges as an antagonistic symbol to the railroad that arrives even as the Kid leads his rag-tag followers through isolated southeastern New Mexico.

Once the scene is set, Burns fully introduces Pat Garrett, figuratively and literally the destroyer of Billy and the disappearing world he represents. Although readers and reviewers sympathetic to Billy in the 1920s—as well as those in more recent times—often criticize Burns for what they consider his downsizing of Billy and his magnification of Pat Garrett, they miss the larger story Burns told. Like so many novelists, historians, and biographers in the half-century from the 1880s to the 1930s, Burns portrayed the West as a closing fron-

Billy the Kid

Billy the Kid, the notorious New Mexico outlaw, became
a widely storied figure after the publication of Walter Noble
Burns's *Saga of Billy the Kid* in 1926. (Courtesy Lincoln
Heritage Trust, Lincoln, New Mexico)

tier. In Burns's narrative, Billy represents the dying Old West and its ways of life falling before the newer, more civilized West of Pat Garrett, hired by the corporate cattlemen to rid their ranges of the likes of Billy and his rustling cronies. When Billy dies before Garrett's gun in the darkened bedroom of Pete Maxwell near midnight on July 14, 1881, he represents a Wild West collapsing before an arising new force of civilization, settlement, and law and order. In this way, Garrett illustrates the other half of Professor Brown's Western Civil War of Incorporation, a central, homogenizing power destroying an individualistic, anarchic frontier. Burns made explicit this interpretation of his story when he wrote to a movie publicity agent that he treated Garrett as a "brave man," giving him "full credit for his courage in the performance of his duty as sheriff in a very dangerous period on that particular part of the frontier."[22] For Burns, Billy the Kid could be an appealing, heroic challenger to law and order, but Pat Garrett represented those who made sure a settled West emerged from earlier, chaotic times.

IN March of 1939 William S. Hart, the aging hero of numerous Western films, emerged briefly from retirement to prepare an eight-minute prologue for the remaking of his final silent film, *Tumbleweeds* (1925). In the new sound prologue, Hart, hat in hand, his voice choked with emotion, his arm sweeping over the backdropped landscape of his California ranch, lamented the passing of the Old West and remembered his joys in telling his stories of the frontier on screen. He recalled "the thrill of it all" and that making Westerns "was as the very breath of life" to him. No star played a more central role than Hart in the early Western. For nearly a generation, from World War I into the 1930s, his vision dominated the Western.

Two months before the re-release of *Tumbleweeds,* the film *Stagecoach,* directed by John Ford and starring John Wayne, appeared in theaters across the country. As the cowboy-outlaw Ringo Kid, Wayne both illustrated the frontier roles that had developed in cinematic Westerns and foreshadowed others to be dramatized in the coming years. In addition to showcasing Wayne's memorable role, *Stagecoach,* in its skillful use of the Monument Valley setting, its blending of heroic and villainous characterizations, and its adroit employment of parody and satire, also served as succinct summary of the filmic West in the first four decades of the twentieth century.[23]

Western films followed paths of development remarkably similar to those that writers of popular western fiction traveled in the first years of the twentieth century. At the same time that authors such as Zane Grey, B. M. Bower, and Max Brand solidified and repeated the fictional format that Wister's *Virginian* introduced in 1902, movie heroes like Broncho Billy Anderson, William S. Hart, and Tom Mix starred in hundreds of Westerns featuring protagonists strikingly resembling their fictional cousins. Indeed, in the case of Zane Grey, several of his novels became obvious sources for films in the teens and twenties. As John Cawelti notes in his authoritative study of formulas in popular culture, Grey and William S. Hart often depicted parallel Wests with good bad men proving their worth in dramatic conflicts with evil villains and demanding physical terrains. Concurrent with Grey's best-selling status from the early teens through the 1920s, Hart played to large, appreciative audiences in such films as *Hell's Hinges* (1916), *The Toll Gate* (1920), and *Tumbleweeds* (1925).[24]

In the 1920s, while Hart and Mix continued their marquee status as highly paid Western stars, producers and directors experimented with other kinds of Westerns. *The Covered Wagon* (1923), *The Iron Horse* (1924), and *North of 36* (1924) enacted, for example, the frontier epic stories of the Oregon Trail, the building of the transcontinental railroad, and a cattle drive north from Texas. Meanwhile, two other longer Westerns, *The Vanishing American* (1925) and *The Wind* (1928), tried to give larger, more sympathetic treatment of Native Americans and women. Altogether, the heroic films featuring Hart and Mix and other stalwarts like Buck Jones and Hoot Gibson, the historical epics, and several other kinds of Westerns made up the most popular genre of the 1920s. Of the 6,660 films screened in the decade, 935 were Westerns, nearly 300 more than the next most popular type.[25]

The arrival of sound in the 1920s brought further changes to the filmic West. If the careers of Bronco Billy and Hart had already ended, the talkies nearly destroyed Tom Mix. But for other stars and for the Western in general, sound was a godsend. The Singing Western, with new heroes such as Gene Autry and Roy Rogers, galloped onto the scene like a runaway horse. These guitar-plucking singers and other forms of B (or low-budget) Westerns, many of them made in the Poverty Row section of Hollywood, allowed only the slightest innovations in the genre. The tight times of the Depression also encouraged directors to follow successful traditions in the Western rather than to take risks. This increasingly rigid adherence to a familiar filmic formula led to restlessness among some directors. Among the discontent was John Ford. His twin desires of not breaking from the ingredients of the well-known Western story but also avoiding the most stylized versions of the narrative helped lead to the filming of *Stagecoach* (1939), one of the most remarkable Western films ever made.

Ford said the impetus for *Stagecoach* came from his reading of Ernest Haycox's short story "A Stage to Lordsburg," which appeared in *Collier's* in April 10, 1937. Modeled somewhat after French writer Guy de Maupassant's earlier

Stagecoach (1939)

Stagecoach (1939), directed by John Ford and starring John Wayne, quickly became a classic cinematic Western.

story "Boule de Suif," Haycox's brief narrative tells the story of a stagecoach load of diverse characters riding east from Arizona to New Mexico territory through dreaded Apache country. Each of the nine characters displays his or her personality during the traumatic ordeal. Ford was particularly attracted to the varied characters who people Haycox's abbreviated story.[26]

The parallels as well as the differences between Haycox's fiction and the screenplay by Dudley Nichols and the film directed by John Ford tell us much about the staying power of the Western, its elasticity, and the importance of Ford and John Wayne to the cinematic West. Both mediums use the popular Western motif of a harrowing journey across rugged terrain. Both utilize the developing love story between the outlaw hero and the prostitute heroine. Both treat the Apache Indians as a deadly threat to the Anglo "civilizing" of the West. And, finally, both depict the trip as a trek through hell toward resolution and possible happiness. In their desire to demonstrate the palpable strengths of the Nichols/Ford film, scholars often underestimate how much Haycox's short story contributed to *Stagecoach*.

The changes are even more notable than the similarities, however. Later, Ford hinted at some of the needed enhancements when he wrote that Haycox's "Stage to Lordsburg" was a "great story" with "great characters in it" but that "it wasn't too well developed." Although seven of Ford's characters—the hero, the prostitute heroine, the gambler, the whiskey drummer, the stage driver, the shotgun guard, and the fiancée (Haycox) or wife (Ford) of the army officer— are taken from Haycox's story, they are much more well developed in the film than in the earlier story. Even larger changes in characterization occur when Haycox's lusting cattleman and wooden English sportsman are replaced in *Stagecoach* with superb roles for a crooked banker (Berton Churchill) and a drunken doctor (Thomas Mitchell). Besides those transformations in the central characters, Ford greatly augmented the power of the setting through his unforgettable evocation of Monument Valley. Nor can we forget Ford's skillful handling of class conflict and his innovative camera work.[27]

Ford's pathbreaking achievements within the boundaries of the Western are especially evident in his relished contradictions, reversals, and ironies. These incongruences and paradoxes abound in *Stagecoach*. In the traditional western story, the hero and heroine usually are moral models for other characters and needy readers, but Ford's leading protagonists are an escaped prisoner, the Ringo Kid (John Wayne), and a prostitute, Dallas (Claire Trevor). Similarly, Doc Boone (Thomas Mitchell) is no upstanding member of the medical elite but a drunk chased out of town by the self-proclaimed agents of moral order, who also drive Dallas from her house of ill repute. The same born-again bigots verbally whip the gambler into leaving on the stagecoach to find a new set of round-table victims.

In Ford's skillful hands none of these characters is as he or she at first appears. Ringo has broken out of jail, for example, but the film implies the Kid is a good man framed by the evil Plummer brothers. Ringo proves his virtue in his love for Dallas, in risking his life for the stagecoach community, and in his destruction of the evil elements of Lordsburg at the end of the film. Like the earlier good/bad men whom Broncho Billy and William S. Hart played in silent Westerns, Ringo regenerates most of those he meets through his essential worth.[28]

In like manner, although Dallas is clearly a prostitute, we learn that the deaths of her parents and economic necessity drove her into the occupation. She says: "Well, you gotta live, no matter what happens." Of all the characters in *Stagecoach*, Dallas displays the most concern for others' needs. She empathizes with the Kid's dilemmas and looks after a baby born to a passenger. But Dallas's nurturing nature exhibits itself most clearly in her aiding the baby's mother, the wife of a soldier on her way to join her husband. Although that expectant and then new mother, bent on maintaining distance between herself and the other woman, initially rejects Dallas's offers of help, when she suddenly goes into labor, it is Dallas and the social outcast, Doc Boone, who successfully midwife the child into life under these difficult, primitive circumstances. Through skillful directing, Ford highlights Dallas not as a wicked whore but as a redemptive, maternal woman. Notable camera work, utilizing the iris effect, focuses on Dallas as she carries the new infant to the travelers. As the camera zeroes in on Dallas, she becomes, in the male gaze of Ringo, an illuminated madonnalike mother, redeemed and newly pure. A cut-away to Ringo reveals his appreciation of Dallas and explains his growing desire to make her his companion on a ranch across the border.

John Ford's most obvious change from Haycox's story came in the addition of Doc Boone to the cast of *Stagecoach*. A drunken sot marvelously played by Thomas Mitchell, for which he deservedly won an Oscar, Doc disgraces his profession, from the perspective of the viragos of the Law and Order League. But in Ford's cinematic calculus, Doc becomes, like Ringo and Dallas, a redeeming figure going about doing good. He calms Dallas's fears, telling her they are "victims of a foul disease called social prejudice"; and later, after apologetically admitting to her "who am I to tell you what's right or wrong," he urges her to find happiness with Ringo. It is Doc who strips away the false facades of Hatfield the gambler and Gatewood the banker. In the final scene, Doc joins Curley the marshall in urging Ringo and Dallas out of Lordsburg, through one example of the film's biting social criticism: "Well, they're saved from the blessings of civilization."

If Ringo, Dallas, and Doc are actually society's best citizens often mistreated as social lepers, other characters masquerade as saints to cover their sinfulness. The banker, who pontificates that "what's good for the banks is good for the country," turns out to be a thief stealing from his own bank. Quite possibly he abandons the town of Tonto because his wife, the fearful leader of the Law and Order League, drives him from his own home. As Dallas stares at these self-righteous reformers, she wryly notes: "There are worse things than Apaches." In less dramatic reversals, the gambler and soldier's wife are so bound to their southern codes of honor they are unable to admit to their dishonor and social prejudice.

Discerning viewers can appreciate these changes as evidences of Ford's innovatively playing with familiar ingredients of the western story in *Stagecoach*. In other ways, the film follows closely the format of the Western. In addition to the villains riding in the stagecoach, the Apaches (played primarily by Navajos) act out the traditional role of menacing opponents in the last leg of the trek eastward. Some of the most spectacular action transpires as the stagecoach careens across the flats with the Indians catching up and threatening to destroy the travelers. In one epiphanic moment, the camera catches Lucy Mallory, the soldier's wife and new mother, praying for deliverance as the Natives race alongside the stagecoach. As she prays, the gambler's pistol appears near her head, revealing his intention of saving her "from a fate worse than death" at the hands of the Apaches. Before Hatfield can pull the trigger, he falls before an Indian shot, and seconds later the sounding bugle charge indicates soldiers have arrived, saving the stagecoach and dispatching the Indians.

No less typical of traditional villains are the roles for the Plummer brothers. We learn they have killed the Kid's father and brother and were instrumental in Ringo's being unjustly imprisoned. Now he has escaped to gain revenge on these evildoers. So driven is Ringo to do in the Plummers that he even keeps back three much-needed bullets in the do-or-die struggle with the Apaches. As he tells Dallas, before they talk of the future, he has "got to go to Lordsburg." "There's some things a man just can't run away from." With these words and in his final victorious shootout with the Plummers on a darkened street in Lordsburg, Ringo echoes the need of the Virginian to kill Trampas and the similar sentiments of hundreds of other heroes of Westerns. Before the hero of the western story can marry the heroine or ride out of the valley, he must dispatch the Trampases, the Plummers, or the Indians that stand in the way of civilization.

John Wayne's stunning depiction of the Ringo Kid in *Stagecoach* greatly magnified its role as a traditional western story as well as elevated its status to what critics called a "superior Western." Wayne's Ringo clearly follows in the long line of western heroes stretching from Buffalo Bill's protagonists to the fictional, biographical, and cinematic mighty men of the early twentieth century. As a courageous, valiant, and naive hero, Ringo helps save the stagecoach community, battles the Apaches, and wipes out the wicked Plummers. True, he's bent on personal revenge, but meanwhile he's willing to risk his life to protect all travelers, including those unworthy of his bravery and valor.

Beyond these common traits expected of a western story hero, Wayne's Ringo also exhibits the best of democratic virtues. He accepts both the upstanding and villainous figures alike among his fellow travelers. He also serves as the mouthpiece for some of John Ford's biting satire. When the socially pretentious members of the group shy away from Dallas and Ringo, he takes their opprobrium (mainly aimed at Dallas) on himself, declaring "Well, I guess you can't break out of prison and into society in the same week." So, in this expansive heart of darkness through which the stagecoach must travel, the hero not only models for the travelers selfless, courageous actions, but also makes possible the journey's end by wiping out those who still threaten society.[29]

Some commentators think *Stagecoach* more an exceptional than a traditional Western. But if one considers how much John Wayne and John Ford dominated Westerns into the 1960s, it's difficult to emphasize primarily the movie's exceptional qualities. Wayne's Ringo is as prologue to his later attention-catching roles in *Red River* (1946), the so-called Cavalry Westerns (*Fort Apache* [1948], *She Wore a Yellow Ribbon* [1949], *Rio Grande* [1950]), and later films such as *The Searchers* (1956), *True Grit* (1969), and *The Shootist* (1976). By the 1940s and throughout the remaining thirty years of his career John Wayne was the country's best-known star of Westerns. And that popularity remained. As late as the mid-1990s a poll of Hollywood's best-loved heroes ranked Wayne at the top of the list.

John Wayne in *Stagecoach*

John Wayne's role as the Ringo Kid in *Stagecoach* (1939) established him as a leading hero of the Western. Here he stands next to Dallas (Claire Trevor), the prostitute heroine of the film.

Meanwhile, John Ford gained and maintained his status as the most-recognized director of Westerns. In fact, he often introduced himself as "John Ford, I make Westerns." For Ford, the Western offered an ideal genre for treating several of the character types, experiences, and settings that interested him. Testing the masculinity and fortitude of frontier soldiers, gunfighters, and settlers particularly intrigued Ford. If these movies could be shot in Monument Valley or in another appealing western setting, all the better for Ford. Living and working in isolated, rural settings with a favored cast always attracted to the famed director.

After *Stagecoach,* Wayne and Ford teamed up for several other Westerns. In addition to working together on the Cavalry Westerns, they labored as a duo in, among others, *The Searchers* (1956), *The Alamo* (1960), and *The Man Who Shot Liberty Valance* (1962). Ford was often a difficult, sometimes an impossible taskmaster as a director. Even Wayne, Ford's best-known Western actor, frequently became the victim of the director's goading, his unfair, even snide tongue lashings. At the same time, Ford turned again and again to Wayne for leading roles in his notable Westerns. More than any other director, Ford made John Wayne a Western star.

Together, John Ford and John Wayne, as director and superstar, dominated the Western for two generations. First in *Stagecoach* and then throughout the 1940s and 1950s and into the 1960s, Ford and Wayne pictured and acted out western stories now familiar to huge audiences of viewers. Their West and its larger-than-life heroes did much to solidify the stereotyped ingredients of the Western by the mid-twentieth century. What Owen Wister, Zane Grey, Ernest Haycox, and Luke Short were to popular fiction, what Frederic Remington and Charles Russell were to popular artistic renderings of the West, John Ford and John Wayne were to the Hollywood West. Together, these important writers, artists, and movie makers paved the way for Louis L'Amour, the most well known of all the popularizers of the western story.

It was an auspicious moment for the western story. Louis L'Amour, the country's best-known writer of popular western fiction, had flown to Washington D.C., to receive a National Gold Medal from Congress. Presenting the medal to L'Amour, President Ronald Reagan saluted the recipient's "enormous contributions to Western folklore and our frontier heritage." Here, on September 24, 1983, America's cinematic cowboy president lionized the U.S.'s leading western popular novelist. The cultural significance of the occurrence may have been lost on most of the participants, but it was of pregnant importance for western storytellers. Just as President Reagan saw himself as restoring American patriotism and older, sometimes frontier values, so L'Amour was convinced that his frontier fiction could serve as a restorative and constructive moral guide for Americans lost in a gray wilderness. Reagan and L'Amour were—and remain—for many Americans symbols of continuity in a world dashing through change.[30]

Louis L'Amour's path to that paradigmatic moment in Washington D.C., in 1983, was neither easy nor direct. Born Louis Dearborn LaMoore in Jamestown, North Dakota, in 1908, L'Amour moved to the Southwest with his family in his mid-teens. Then, leaving home, he began several years of wandering, or "yondering" as he later termed his vagabond years. After serving four years in World War II, L'Amour turned to writing full time. Publishing dozens of adventure stories, L'Amour also wrote four Hopalong Cassidy novels as Tex Burns (1950–1952) before his best-selling *Hondo* appeared in 1953.

In several ways, Louis L'Amour was the notable exception to most trends in western storytelling in the post-1960 years. Even though the traditional Western, in fiction and film, fell on hard times during the late 1960s and the 1970s, L'Amour's novels sold by the millions. So phenomenal were his sales that his publisher Bantam Books could keep all his eighty-plus novels in print and count on sales of at least a million copies for every new L'Amour volume it published. Experimenting with length, format, and, eventually, subject matter, L'Amour far outsold any other writer of Westerns and became one of the all-time, best-selling American writers. As John Wayne had earlier in the film Western, L'Amour became known around the world for his fictional portraits of the American frontier.

Hondo, L'Amour's first novel published in the United States under his own name, illustrates how quickly he became known as a new producer of the western story. Beginning his career in the 1930s writing primarily adventure stories about the Far East, L'Amour turned to the frontier and American West full time in the late 1940s. When L'Amour's short story "The Gift of Cochise" (1952) caught the attention of James Edward Grant, a screenwriter, he did a screenplay of the story, which Warner Brothers released in 3-D format starring John Wayne. In some way, L'Amour gained permission to novelize the screenplay and even talked John Wayne into puffing the novel without having read it. When the film and novel were released simultaneously in November 1953,

L'Amour's fiction gained valuable attention and sales from the positive reaction to Wayne's film. Fawcett, L'Amour's publisher, printed 320,000 copies of the novel and blitzed the public with posters, cards, and bulletins emphasizing the movie tie-in. Sales for the novel skyrocketed. In fact, *Hondo* remains L'Amour's best-selling novel, having sold nearly three million copies by the late 1990s.[31]

Hondo reflects how much L'Amour followed the familiar content and form of the western story as it had evolved by the mid-twentieth century. L'Amour's hero, introduced in the opening sentences, clearly stands in the Virginian tradition:

> He rolled the cigarette in his lips, liking the taste of the tobacco, squinting his eyes against the sun glare. His buckskin shirt, seasoned by the sun, rain, and sweat, smelled stale and old. . . . He was a big man, wide-shouldered, with the lean, hard-boned face of the desert rider. There was no softness in him. His toughness was ingrained and deep, without cruelty, yet quick, hard, and dangerous. (1)

L'Amour's Hondo Lane is a direct literary descendant of Zane Grey's Lassiter, Max Brand's Dan Barry, and the sun-bronzed heroes of Ernest Haycox and Luke Short. These are courageous, direct, never-give-an-inch, masculine heroes who dominate the story lines of the novels they inhabit.

These mighty men must be bold, individualistic, and powerful because they face a challenging landscape, worthy opponents, and evil villains. Hondo appeals to Angie Lowe, the heroine, as a man "who knew himself, knew his strength and his weakness, who measured himself against the hard land of his living, against the men of that land, and against its wilderness" (28). But the hero learns, as do all of L'Amour's successful men, not to directly confront the coercive southwestern setting but to study it, to understand how to live within its strictures. Having lived with the Apache for several years, Hondo also knows the secrets of living off the sparse terrain.

But the hero's victories are not easily won. He must be constantly wary, keeping his keen senses alive to continued threats. In fact, the plot of *Hondo* suggests that a successful Western often parallels the scenario of a deeply flawed marriage. Persisting tension leads to alienation, to conflict, and then to a series of sometimes violent confrontations. L'Amour's *Hondo* follows the format. The novel opens with a faulty marriage in which Ed Lowe has virtually abandoned the faithful Angie and their son Johnny. When the hero encounters the marooned wife, she is drawn to him and he to her, much as the wife and hero

Hondo (1952)

The celebrated appearance of *Hondo* (1952) launched Louis L'Amour's career as a notable western storyteller. (Fawcett Gold Medal reprint)

are in the fictional and cinematic *Shane.* Following his own preachments about fictional storytelling, L'Amour creates scene after scene of action and tension. He keeps the anxiousness between Hondo and Angie at high pitch and then intensifies the emotional level when Hondo encounters the faithless Ed Lowe. The author adds still another thread of conflict to these continuing tensions when he sends the Apaches and soldiers against one another—dramatic events occurring alongside the broken marriage and love affair engulfing the Lowes and Hondo.[32]

If much of the content and form of *Hondo* are familiar fare, his treatment of Indians differs noticeably from their depictions early in the century. Although Native Americans in *Hondo,* along with evil white men, serve as the major antagonists, they are not pictured as brutal savages bent on rape and pillage. As one critic notes, L'Amour sees good and bad in Indians, views their culture as often opposing (but not necessarily less viable than) white culture, and accepts the belief that human history has always included the migrations and invasions of new, more powerful societies. In *Hondo,* Hondo Lane is racially part Indian, he's been married to an Indian woman, and for several years he lived with the Apache. Unlike the Buffalo Bill figure of earlier times who served as scout and cultural outrider, as the vanguard of American invasion, Hondo links Apache and Anglo cultures. He speaks their language, learns their wilderness lore and wisdom, and teaches those lessons to young Johnny Lowe. True, there are bad men like Silva among the Indians, but it is the human and wise Vittoro who values the bravery of Hondo and Angie and adopts Johnny as his blood son.

No one should credit Louis L'Amour, however, for being the first western storyteller to provide a more humane portrait of Indians, especially the much-maligned Apaches. L'Amour's contemporaries, Henry Wilson Allen (Will Henry) and Alan LeMay were producing more complex and sometimes more favorable treatments of Native Americans, and the film *Broken Arrow* (1950) also provided a positive image of Indians. Meanwhile, historians in the 1950s and 1960s were beginning to drop the "savage" description of Indians and essaying monographs treating Indian-white relations in a more balanced and probing fashion. Throughout his career, L'Amour displayed this more humane attitude toward Indians. Although L'Amour's Native Americans might be opponents, they might be tenacious fighters, and they might follow different codes of action and behavior, they were never the brutal redskins of the dime novel Western.[33]

L'Amour quickly took advantage of the successes of *Hondo*. Winning a contract for a novel a year from Fawcett, he soon asked for a new agreement for two books annually. When the publisher refused to accede to his request, he signed an agreement with Bantam for two novels a year (later expanded to three novels). L'Amour's career took off in the 1960s and 1970s when he averaged nearly three novels a year. Along with the financial success came his interest in (and his publisher's willingness) to cautiously experiment with the content and format of his frontier and western stories.

In 1960, L'Amour published *The Daybreakers,* the first book in his multi-volume Sackett family saga. Before his death in 1988, L'Amour had completed seven books about the migrating Sackett tribe. To these stories of immigrating Englishmen he added five novels about the Irish Chantrys and the French Talons. L'Amour sketched out dozens more of the family novels but finished only twenty-five. A few months before his death, he wrote that he tried to use the stories of the Sacketts, Chantrys, and Talons to "tell the story of the opening of a continent as seen through the eyes of three families."[34] If *Hondo* dramatizes the story of the lone individual fighting off nearly overwhelming odds and migrating to another, less chaotic locale, the family saga novels tell of the peopling, the settling, and the growth of the frontier and American West.

Appearing a quarter century after *Hondo, Bendigo Shafter* (1979), one of L'Amour's best novels, represents the author's many fictions treating the initial settling and community building in the American West. Although not part of the family sagas, this novel treats many of the same themes found, for example, in the Sackett series. Set in the early 1860s and following years in the isolated, rugged South Pass area of Wyoming territory, this sprawling novel encompasses a much larger cast of characters and much broader spectrum of ideas and setting than usually inhabit one of L'Amour's novels. As one authority on western writing has argued, *Bendigo Shafter* "is unquestionably one of L'Amour's most significant productions."[35]

Most of all, this novel depicts the trials and errors involved in attempting to build a frontier community. In this regard, *Bendigo Shafter* dramatizes in one novel the three stages of development that L'Amour's families usually represent: the Sacketts (first settlers), the Talons (builders), and Chantrys (thinkers or intellectuals).[36] Through the consciousness of the eponymous hero we see the first rude settlements lurch toward a community. Through Bendigo (who matures to Ben) Shafter, we see one representation of the experience and knowledge pioneers must gain before they become community-minded. More than

Bendigo Shafter (1979)

Bendigo Shafter (1979) illustrates Louis L'Amour's fascination with coming-of-age heroes who learn much from their demanding environments, their families, and older men and women. (Bantam Books, Cover Art Lou Glanzman)

from many of L'Amour's other novels, readers also gain a clear indication of what approaching manhood demands of the hero. Here too are several types of heroines and their varied relationships with men and the nascent community. At the same time, L'Amour provides a fuller portrait of Native Americans, including glimpses of the mystical nature of Indian beliefs. *Bendigo Shafter* likewise overflows with its creator's favorite bromides about the frontier and its sociocultural characteristics.

Eighteen-year-old Ben Shafter, although younger than most of L'Amour's heroes, nonetheless exhibits most of the virtues of the novelist's leading men. From the opening pages, where the story begins with Ben's "we" and "I," he hungers and thirsts after learning, whether from experience or books. Repeatedly L'Amour defines his protagonists as men driven to "learn," "think," and "see." As the alpha and omega of a L'Amour hero, in fact of all good men and true, Ben epitomizes what one can learn and "'what he creates to leave behind.'" None of the best-known authors of popular Westerns, including Owen Wister, B. M. Bower, Max Brand, Ernest Haycox, or Luke Short, was so compelled as L'Amour to make his or her major protagonists such clear reflections of their personal experiences or focused reading. Nearly a half-century earlier, well before L'Amour published his first books, he wrote to well-known American folklorist B. A. Botkin, revealing how much he intended to write out of his personal experience. Until his final novels L'Amour seemed convinced that what he had learned as a self-made, self-educated man should be the essence of what his fiction conveyed.[37]

In *Bendigo Shafter,* the young hero carries a heavy load of the author's autobiographical freight. Like his creator, Ben relishes books and ideas, constantly thinks and plans the future, and travels to educate himself. He ponders the frictions between individualism and community-building, the differences between Indian and white cultures, and the nourishing ingredients of a sound family— all staples of many L'Amour stories. In fact, L'Amour often overloads Ben with authorial intrusion. Frequently, Ben's musings quickly become the author's preachments: "The more I'd read and observed [Ben begins] the more I realized that the best intentions in the world will get a man just nowhere unless he knows how to get results and can enlist the cooperation of others. And cooperation means compromise" (200). Although carping critics pointed to these unwarranted entrances as major weaknesses in L'Amour's fiction, his loyal readers cherished these moments of observation and reflection as part and parcel of his appealing role as a campfire storyteller.

Ben also learns a good deal from the women he encounters. Even though no woman in this novel plays the leading role that Mary Breyton takes in *The Cherokee Trail* (1982), several do fill important parts. Flirtatious teenager Mae Stuart teaches Ben the dangers of sexual attraction before he's sufficiently mature. He also realizes the burdens of wives and young mothers from his sister-in-law Helen. Likewise, the quick maturation of his younger sister Lorna convinces Ben that, like all women, she wants "children, a husband, church on Sunday, the shade of trees, the beauty of flowers. . . . She was one of the good ones who would rear strong sons who would walk their way in pride of home, of country, and of pleasure in their families" (187). For L'Amour (and for Ben Shafter), women are nest builders, and no man should consider marriage until he can provide his wife with home and hearth.

Two other women play even more significant roles in *Bendigo Shafter*. Widow Ruth Macken, beautiful and still in her twenties, becomes Ben's intellectual mentor. More than any other person she looks after his education, providing him with books and challenging him to think about his circumstances. She is accorded, unlike most heroines in traditional Westerns, equal status with the townsmen as a community builder. Ruth Macken, Ben tells us, "was important" to him; "she had set a standard of womanhood against which every woman I later was to know would be unconsciously measured." Not only was she "quietly beautiful, moving with an easy grace and confidence," she was also "tolerant, understanding, and intelligent" (299, 300). Macken is, in short, an ideal woman—the equivalent of the more numerous ideal men who inhabit L'Amour's western stories.

But it's Ninon Vauvert, the girl-woman, to whom Ben is romantically attracted. In some ways Ninon is, like Ruth Macken, an unusual young woman for a traditional Western. A precocious preteen and, like Shafter, an orphan, Ninon resembles L'Amour's young heroes in her desire to experience and learn. Even at twelve, she kisses Ben goodbye before his long trip, telling him she loves him and "'Someday I shall marry you'" (127). L'Amour conveniently keeps Ben and Ninon apart as they mature and find themselves, yet the novel's closing line indicates that Ben, after experiencing a moment of epiphany in the mountains, will go "back to Ninon and the life that lay" before them (323).[38]

Bendigo Shafter also suggests how far the western story had moved away from depicting Indians as merely the "savage" other of the wilderness. In the novel, Native Americans appear first as competition, as a people fighting to save land they inhabited earlier. One young Native, driven by his expectant warrior status, represents the vicious Plains Indian opponent throughout the novel. But, as L'Amour did in *Hondo* and in many of his other stories, he provides a wise, older Indian to balance the young warrior. Old Uruwishi, a Umatilla from the Pacific Northwest whose memory stretches back to Lewis and Clark's journey through the area, becomes something of a guru for Ben Shafter. The young frontiersman learns as much from the old Indian as from his white mentors and their books. Indeed, in the final trip in the novel, Uruwishi, Ben, and other companions journey to the top of Wyoming's Big Horn Mountains to visit a Medicine Wheel, a sacred site for Indians and a site that holds mystic promise for Ben. On that journey Ben must kill the young warrior, but he also achieves a new self-understanding at the Wheel. As Uruwishi dies at this sacred place, Ben inherits a portion of his knowledge and wisdom.

In several of the novel's scenes, L'Amour uses more than one character to comment on Indian-white differences. Early on, a few settlers wish to kill the young Indian who has threatened them, but others realize that this young warrior and his band live by different codes of honor. These pioneers counsel patience and understanding rather than confrontation and conflict. Not surprisingly, Ben Shafter speaks often and much like L'Amour on other occasions. On a trip east, Ben chances to meet famed newspaperman Horace Greeley and tells him that "'most white men do not understand the Indian, [and] many do not think it important to try. They simply accept the Indian as an obstacle to settlement of the land, just as the buffalo is.'" But, Shafter adds, whites need to realize that as long as Natives follow the traditions of a warrior society, they will attack newcomers—to attain honor, to count coups. The problem, succinctly stated, "'is simply that we have two peoples face to face with different religious beliefs, different customs, different styles of living. . . . Before there can be peace there must be a new code of values for the Indian, and such things take generations to develop'" (260–61). Adding to the difficulty, Ben tells Ninon on another occasion, is an immutable truism of the past: "'Wherever two cultures collide, the one with the most efficient way of living will survive'" (256).[39]

These conflicts with Indians and the eventual victory of the whites are but part of L'Amour's story of winning the West. As other western storytellers had been doing for more than a century, L'Amour shows the pioneers continuously tested in their tenacious efforts to establish a stable community on an isolated frontier. Shortly after the dreadful buffeting of a numbing blizzard, the settlers must drive off renegades bent on stealing their women. A few days later they are called upon to take on the burden of a group of starving, unsuccessful over-landers. Perhaps the most difficult barriers to surmount, however, arise from the stubborn, even zealous, ideologues and trouble makers among them or that soon invade their inchoate settlement.

This series of tests, as well as dozens of others, allows L'Amour to portray the frontier West as a contest arena. Thinking back over his life in the nascent community of South Pass City, Ben Shafter, echoing the career-long sentiments of his literary creator, concludes, "the Indians would kill some of the new-comers. Cold, starvation, drought, and storm would kill others, but there would be no end for they would still come." "Men move across the face of the world like tides upon the sea," Ben muses, "and when they have gone, others will come; and the weak would pass and the strong would live, for that was the way it was, and the way it would be" (288). South Pass City will grow stronger through these testings because Ben and his friends, Ruth Mackin, and other like-minded settlers, trading away some of their individualism, will devote their energies to build a surviving frontier community in the midst of a demand-ing physical environment and among disparate and sometimes contentious hu-mans. This was the central theme of *Bendigo Shafter,* as it was for most of Louis L'Amour's stories of the American frontier and West.

Published at the beginning and near the end of L'Amour's novel-writing ca-reer, *Hondo* and *Bendigo Shafter* not only illustrate the major ingredients of his western stories, they also epitomize the varieties of story formats he utilized. In the earlier stages of his career, L'Amour wrote primarily brief stories focused on the deeds of a few brave men. *Hondo* and the Sackett and other family saga novels are of this type. But later, L'Amour wrote several longer, more complex historical novels. *Bendigo Shafter* represents these more ambitious fictional ef-forts. Earlier, *Sitka* (1957) and later *The Comstock Lode* (1981), *The Lonesome Gods* (1983), *The Walking Drum* (1984), *Last of the Breed* (1986), and *The Haunted Mesa* (1987) serve as examples of the longer, less formula ridden, and more historical fiction of L'Amour. *The Walking Drum,* set in twelfth-century Europe and the Far East, and *Last of the Breed,* an adventure story of contem-porary Russia, suggest L'Amour's willingness to experiment with nonwestern settings.[40]

One can easily make too much of these differences, however. Predictable plots, familiar heroes and heroines, and similar conflicts and conclusions count much more than tinkering changes in form and theme in understanding L'Amour's western stories. L'Amour, whom *Time* magazine half-seriously labeled the "Homer of the Oater,"[41] discovered after an apprenticeship in the pulps that he could tell lively, well-plotted, adventure stories about the frontier that attracted thousands of readers. Through more than ninety novels, L'Amour featured courageous and ambitious heroes who fight against coercive physical environments usually peopled with Indian opponents and villainous white men to prove their valor and worth. If that story line sounds familiar, it should, for writers, film-makers, and artists had utilized it for more than a century in telling their western stories.

But L'Amour, in terms of popularity, became the most successful of all western storytellers. Perhaps his best-selling status in the conservative decades of the 1950s and 1980s seems understandable. Yet his books sold as well in the less traditional 1960s and 1970s. Indeed, even as dozens of authors, including novelists, historians, and biographers, were revising the western past, L'Amour continued to publish two or three novels a year that refused to follow these new trends. On numerous occasions, scholars and critics attempted to shoot L'Amour out of his saddle of popular prominence by accusing him of perpetuating a false myth of a heroic frontier. Although L'Amour claimed to pay no attention to his critics, he sometimes attempted to undercut their views. For example, in one of his novels, a character is described as becoming "impatient with those [in the East] who spoke with tolerant smiles of the West, or of what they referred to as 'the western myth.' Back of every myth," L'Amour continues, "there is a stern, harsh reality shaped by men and women of truly heroic mold. Those soft-bellied ones who come later find it easy to refer to things beyond their own grasp as myth."[42] Above all, Louis L'Amour was convinced he told the truth about the frontier past, that his fiction was realistic, that his stories were based on a real, historical West. Millions of readers agreed. By the end of the twentieth century, nearly 250 million copies of his novels and short stories had sold, making him the best-selling western storyteller of all time.

ALTHOUGH Louis L'Amour far surpassed in popularity and sales any other western author, he was not the whole story in the second half of the twentieth century. In fact, his career, especially after the 1960s, was the major exception to trends in western storytelling during this period. Even before L'Amour dashed upon the scene, novelists, biographers, and film-makers, tired of the western story formula, produced parodies and satires of that familiar narrative. And, as early as the late 1920s, regionalists all over the West called for a new, more inclusive way of telling western stories. They urged writers to break out of what they considered the excessively romantic, stereotyped attachments to the frontier and, instead, to deal with the cultural complexities of a postfrontier West. Two generations later, other pundits began calling on authors to pay much more attention to racial, ethnic, women's, and environmental influences in their western stories. Even as Louis L'Amour gained in popularity, other writers broke from the earlier restrictive storylines stretching back to the dime novelists. Through their re-visionings the regionalists and the post-1950s writers told New Stories about the American West.

Chapter Four

New Stories

WHEN Walter Van Tilburg Clark's notable novel *The Ox-Bow Incident* appeared in 1940, reviewers and readers seemed uncertain how to react. Clark's book featured a frontier setting and several recognizable pioneer types, but its plot, including the vigilante hanging of sheepherders, lengthy conversations about illegal violence, and unheroic characters, broke repeatedly from the familiar formula of the traditional western story. For many, Clark's novel seemed more an answer to *The Virginian* than a recognizable Western.

The Ox-Bow Incident was but one of many novels, films, and histories and biographies that challenged the format of the western story. At much the same time, two other novels, H. L. Davis's *Honey in the Horn* (1935), and John Steinbeck's *The Grapes of Wrath* (1939), also contested the plot lines of the Western. The cinematic versions of *The Ox-Bow Incident* (1942) and *Grapes of Wrath* (1940) added to these challenges. And by the 1950s and 1960s, Henry Nash Smith's invaluable study *Virgin Land: The American West as Symbol and Myth* (1950) and Don Russell's thorough, fact-filled biography, *The Lives and Legends of Buffalo Bill* (1960), were further exceptions to the Wild West story line.

Other writers and film-makers raised questions through the less confrontational means of humor and satire. From the teens to World War II, authors such as B. M. Bower, Max Brand, W. C. Tuttle, among many others, attempted to undercut, with humor, the cult of the larger-than-life Western hero. Journalist/historian Duncan Aikman did the same with his satirical treatments of several Wild West heroines in *Calamity Jane and the Lady Wildcats* (1927). Meanwhile, silent actors like Mack Sennett, Buster Keaton, and Laurel and Hardy satirized familiar "platitudes, villainy, and action" in dozens of comic and slapstick Westerns. Later, Abbott and Costello, Bob Hope, and Jack Benny also found much to parody in the Western.[1]

The most powerful challenges to the western story came not from critiques and satires of the narrative, however, but from regionalists surfacing in the 1920s and 1930s. Throughout the interwar years and well past World War II, regionalists called for a new kind of story line about the American West. Discontent with plots that too often focused on a frontier of clash and conflict, regional editors, novelists, and a few historians urged writers to stop writing sensational yarns about movement *to* the West and take up stories set *in* the West. Well-known editors B. A. Botkin (*Folk-Say*), H. G. Merrian (*Frontier*), John H. McGinnis (*Southwest Review*), and John T. Frederick (*The Midland*) took up the cudgels for a regionalism that portrayed the shaping power of physical and cultural environments, over time, within specific subregions of the West.[2]

Throughout the West, from the 1920s to the early 1960s, regionalists championed this counter-narrative to the Wild West or frontier story. Some of the editors urged their contributors to collect the lore and history of Native Americans rather than viewing Indians simply as opponents of a Euro-American movement. Other writers sounded the tocsin for treating the contemporary West instead of limiting western stories to frontier contact and turmoil. Since the histories and cultures of the West included pre-contact, pioneer, and post-frontier periods, these commentators argued, novelists and historians must tell the full story of cultural transformations within western subregions. They must demonstrate how unique character types and ideas emerged from specific locations within the West. The birth and florescence of this redolent western regionalism paralleled a similar movement that concurrently invaded the South.

Western regionalism stretched over two generations. In the first generation two women writers, Mary Austin and Willa Cather, emphasized the desert Southwest and the agricultural Midwest to dramatize interactions between these settings and humans residing there. Serving as unifying links between the two generations of western writers, regional editors in the 1920s and 1930s became cheerleaders for hosts of later regional writers scattered throughout the West. In the Pacific Northwest, H. L. Davis, Vardis Fisher, and A. B. Guthrie, Jr.; in the Midwest, Ruth Suckow, Frederick Manfred, and historian James Malin; in the Southwest, historian Walter Prescott Webb, folklorist J. Frank Dobie, and novelist Harvey Fergusson; and in California, John Steinbeck—all these writers and several more gained national reputations for their regional fictional and historical writings. Cather and Steinbeck were the major leaders of these two generations of regionalists challenging frontier stories between 1910 and 1950. Then, novelist, biographer, and essayist Wallace Stegner appeared in the 1940s and 1950s and became an increasingly important regionalist, and more, before his death in the early 1990s.[3]

When Stegner's superb novel *Angle of Repose* (1971) won the Pulitzer Prize for fiction, the award signaled a high point of an already illustrious career. Although Stegner published his initial stories and novel in the 1930s, he continued to produce major fiction, histories and biographies, and essays and books on conservation/environmental topics for another half-century. Some authorities on the West consider Stegner the preeminent western writer, whereas others see him as competing with such writers as Cather and Steinbeck for those laurels; but nearly all historians and literary scholars place him among the most prominent western storytellers. In his long, productive career, Stegner provided a memorable example of westerners who broke from the continuing fascination with the frontier West and gravitated toward a more complex regional West. In the last decades of his life, he became a model for novelists and historians wishing to portray the western past as a much more complicated, even messy, subject than writers from Owen Wister to Louis L'Amour had presented.[4]

Wallace Stegner was reared on the tailends of the American and Canadian frontiers, but he always pitched his tent among the regionalists. Nearly all his writing contested the earlier frontier stories of the American West. In his first widely reviewed novel, *The Big Rock Candy Mountain* (1943), he made clear his life-long predilections. Hailed as a sprawling, picaresque story of the twentieth-century West, the novel, Stegner admitted, was "family history reasonably straight." The author's parents served as apt models for the stunning portraits of Bo Mason—booming, restless, wandering husband—and Elsa Mason— nesting, reluctant, and peace-loving wife dragged throughout the Far West. Here was the first installment of Stegner's western narrative, a superb novel bursting with the stark story of a questing family crisscrossing the two Wests early in the twentieth century, searching for stasis and meaning.[5]

In the 1950s and 1960s Stegner continued publishing in several areas. His story collections, *The Women on the Wall* (1950) and *City of the Living* (1956), illustrated his first-rank abilities in short fiction, and his *Beyond the Hundredth Meridian: John Wesley Powell and the Second Opening of the West* (1954) remains the soundest guide to Powell's career. Meanwhile, Stegner was finding his environmental voice, and in a series of essays and books from the 1950s onward

Wallace Stegner

Wallace Stegner was often considered the dean of western storytellers from the 1960s until his death in 1993. (Courtesy Mary Page Stegner)

became a leading advocate of more thoughtful approaches to and uses of western lands and landscapes. Of central importance was Stegner's "Wilderness Letter" (1960), a ringing call for a new appreciation of the "wilderness idea." His plea for wilderness rightly viewed as "the geography of hope" has become *the* catch phrase for the modern environmental movement. Meanwhile, Stegner's career as a novelist, so promisingly launched with *Big Rock Candy Mountain*, seemed stalled.[6]

But that all changed dramatically when *Angle of Repose* (1971) appeared to high praise and won the Pulitzer Prize in 1972. Stegner's premier novel not only garnered international acclaim, it built on traditions already established in western regional fiction, linked them to new interpretations of the American West, and produced a new kind of western story. Nearly thirty years later, *Angle of Repose* remains a rich, valuable paradigm for those who wish to escape the earlier western narrative that boxed in so many writers in the previous century.[7]

On one level, *Angle of Repose* is the story of an eastern woman, Susan Burling Ward, who goes west. After marrying another easterner, Oliver Ward, she moves throughout the West, trying to acclimate herself to western ways. This part of Stegner's novel draws heavily on the life and career of noted writer and artist Mary Hallock Foote (Chapter Two). On another level, the book is the story of Susan's grandson, Lyman Ward, a retired historian, an amputee alienated from his world of the late 1960s.

These layered levels allow Stegner to tell a more complex story of the West. By shifting back and forth between Susan's life in the late nineteenth century to Lyman's in the 1960s, Stegner invokes a full century of western history. He works on a huge, complex canvas. But two major themes of western history unify his large picture: (1) what is the relationship between the American East and West? Are there more continuities or changes?; and (2) what comparisons and contrasts can be made between the frontier West and the New West of the 1960s? Revealingly, these two large questions at the center of *Angle of Repose* were also ones western historians were simultaneously raising.[8]

The largest shaping influence of the East on the West is dramatized in the life of Susan Burling Ward. Following her husband from mining camps in California and Colorado, to the new community of Boise, and on to Grass Valley, Susan lives more than a half-century in the West without becoming a contented westerner. She continues to hold on to eastern, genteel symbols. Her clothing, her maid, and governess (perhaps the only household in Boise in the

Angle of Repose (1971)

    Angle of Repose (1971) won the Pulitzer Prize for fiction. It is a complex historical narrative celebrated for its realistic treatment of regional material. (Doubleday & Company, Garden City, New York; jacket by E.D.N. Studio)

1880s to have both), her eastern literary friends, and her allusions to the East and classical tastes—all these symbolize her connections to the East.

Through adroit use of symbolic action Stegner depicts how much Susan is a stranger to western ways. On one occasion, Susan, while standing on an elevated porch and speaking to a Mexican worker, drops her handkerchief. The laborer quickly retrieves it and hands it up to her. Susan reaches down for the handkerchief but suddenly withdraws her hand when she realizes what she is doing. Revealingly displayed is her class bias. She cannot—in fact will not—take the handkerchief from his hand; finally she calls her maid to get it back. Another night, when she and Oliver are returning to Leadville—Colorado's riproaring mining town—they are forced to bed down in a flophouse. Oliver hesitates because he realizes that his wife is horrified at the prospect of sleeping in a curtained-off section of a room within snoring and belching distance of rough miners and dirty vagabonds. Queasy about the situation, Susan lies awake most of the night—first in fear and then, true to her character, in dreaming about how she will picture this "rough" West for eastern magazines. Obviously much of the truth will be brushed away and large doses of romanticism applied before the "dreamed up" West will be publishable in *Century* and *Scribner's*.

A third scene reveals how much Stegner's story focuses on Susan's nonwestern perspective. Before this scene occurs, Oliver and Susan argued about the suitability of an eastern man who has come west. Greatly impressed with the man's reading and his obvious exposure to eastern culture, Susan declares him a cultivated gentleman and is amazed and upset when Oliver says the man is worthless in the West—in fact a hazard—because he knows so little about mining and engineering. One night soon after this discussion Susan and Oliver sit down to dinner, and she mentally criticizes Oliver for not washing before eating—there appears to be a smudge on his thumb. Later, a third person tells of the day's happenings (the account does not come from Oliver, for, as Susan says, he does not like talkee, talkee). Oliver, the eastern engineer, and others were in the mines when someone shouted a warning. The easterner froze, and had not Oliver moved quickly the gentleman might have been killed. The smudge on Oliver's thumb is an ugly, painful bruise suffered from aiding a man whom he does not respect. At the end of the scene, readers realize—as does Susan—how much her viewpoint prevents her from understanding the West and what it demands from its residents.

Breaking from the format of many traditional western stories, Stegner places major emphasis on an eastern woman's inability to find a home in the West. He catches Susan's dilemmas in one ironic sentence: "There sat Susan Burling Ward, tired-eyed after a day's drawing, dragged-out after a day's heat, and tightening her drowning-woman's grip on culture, literature, civilization, by trying to read *War and Peace*" (421). Like the local colorist she is, Susan loves the scenery, the wild and picturesque part of the Boise valley; but once she faces having to live "in" the Boise area, she is repulsed by its remoteness and materialism. Living there seems acceptable only by withdrawal, so she and Oliver and their children move up a river canyon where she tries to establish a western miniature of Brook Farm.[9]

Despite herself, Susan gradually becomes attached to the West. In depicting this gradual accommodation, Stegner moves beyond frontier to regional storyline, showing how a woman, not a man, is redefined in a setting heretofore alien to her. After a series of family conflicts and tragedies, Susan almost gives up on the West and her marriage. But she cannot remain in the East where she has sought emotional and cultural refuge. Something draws her back west again—to Oliver, to disappointments, to other psychological buffetings. She realizes, in spite of herself, that she has become attached to things in the West—even if she is not yet a westerner.

Stegner presents Oliver not as the exact opposite of Susan, as the archetypal westerner, but he does take on characteristics ascribed to many westerners. For example, because Oliver realizes the need for help in achieving his dreams, he is less class-conscious than his wife; he evaluates a person more by abilities than by cultural achievements. Although Oliver is overly protective of his wife, he does not allow an excessive gentility to blind him to western realities that demand a ruggedness and courage unknown to Susan's eastern friends.

Nor is Oliver a local colorist caught up in the picturesque, picnic West. For him, the West is a place to conquer, where he can try out his dreams. Not surprisingly, then, he finds Susan's classical allusions to miners and their arduous work "about used up" (139). On a few occasions Susan realizes that Oliver is different: "It was his physical readiness, his unflusterable way of doing what was needed in a crisis, that she most respected in him: it made him different from the men she had known" (234).

Stegner also uses Oliver to illustrate historian Bernard DeVoto's description of the West as a "plundered province."[10] Oliver works hard in many of his engineering assignments, but he cannot bring his dreams to fruition. Like many

other westerners, he is dependent upon eastern capital; that financing is as untrustworthy as Lady Fortuna. All of Oliver's dreams prove workable—but only
after he has left the scene and sound financing is secured. Oliver's schemes and
partial successes are destroyed because he remains under the lion's paw of un-
dependable eastern money.

Sometimes through the narrator Lyman Ward and sometimes as omniscient
author, Stegner comments on the powerful linkages between East and West.
Early in the novel Lyman says: "I am impressed with how much of my grandparents' life depended on continuities, contacts, connections, friendships, and
blood relationships. Contrary to myth, the West was not made entirely by pioneers who had thrown everything away but an ax and a gun" (41). These realistic observations are often contrasted with Susan's romantic perceptions of
the West. By dramatizing these two notions of the West, Stegner makes clear
how much eastern visions defined what the West meant to most Americans.
Most of these foreign interpreters overstressed the uniqueness and wildness
of western life and underplayed continuities between East and West. The major
point that *Angle of Repose* makes about East-West linkages is the central thesis of Henry Nash Smith's brilliant book *Virgin Land* and among the most significant contributions in the writings of western historian Earl Pomeroy.[11]

The second notable achievement of Stegner's novel is the connection he
forges between the frontier West and the Bay Area counterculture of the 1960s.
In keeping two centuries of western history before readers and in commenting
on transitions between the two periods, Stegner presents a complex view of the
historical development of the West. Throughout the novel, the life and mores
of Susan and Oliver Ward are placed alongside the Berkeley fever of Lyman's
young neighbor, Shelley Rasmussen, and of his son, Rodman. Lyman links the
two periods. As he says: "I really would like to talk to somebody about my
grandparents, their past, their part in the West's becoming, their struggle toward ambiguous ends" (50). Lyman ironically notes the actions of Shelley, a
descendant of a Cornish miner, in helping him interpret the meaning of his
family who "ruled" her ancestors. More to the point, it is a Trevithick (Shelly's
mother) who, more than any of Lyman's kin, keeps him moving physically.
Stegner's story implies that the social and cultural history of the West has lev-
eled mountains, elevated valleys, and bridged several class chasms.

From Lyman Ward, narrator, commentator, and synthesizer, one learns most
about history. It is he who connects the frontier and the New West. From the
novel's opening pages, Stegner establishes a fluidity of time, with Lyman

switching from present to past and back to the present as he searches for an understanding of his life. In these syncopations of time, Lyman perceives paradoxical truths: as soon as he experiences the *present*, it is the past; he is *in* and *of* the past just as he is tied to a complicated present. In his attempt to comprehend fully the relationships between the Old and New Wests, Lyman utilizes two geological terms. The first is "angle of repose," the level of incline at which rocks cease to fall. The second term, the Doppler Effect, defines how he wishes to undertake his study of past and present. To understand the "angle of repose" Susan and Oliver Ward reached in their lives, Lyman must not view his grandparents from the 1960s but must place himself alongside them, living his life alongside theirs. Stegner pictures Lyman as wishing to avoid presentism and to become instead a past-minded historian, reliving his grandparents' lives with understanding and objectivity.

Several pressures keep Lyman from telling the kinds of stories he wishes to narrate. For one, few of his contemporaries value his research subjects or methods. To Lyman, the Berkeley generation seem "without the sense of history. . . . [To them] it is only an aborted social science." His son Rodman sums up the view that his father fears: "The past isn't going to teach us anything about what we've got ahead of us. Maybe it did once, or seemed to. It doesn't anymore." Lyman believes just the opposite; the past, he argues, is "the only direction we can learn from." He continues: "I believe in Time, as they [his grandparents] did, and in life chronological rather than in life existential. We live in time and through it, we build our huts in its rivers, or used to, and we cannot afford all these abandonings" (15–16, 17, 18). Rodman's generation, Lyman thinks, has not yet learned this lesson; the youth of the 1960s, he says, are "by Paul Goodman out of Margaret Mead"(18).

Sounding like his creator, Lyman also wants to avoid a distorted meaning of the past. Too many readers are like his son Rodman, who wants history to bubble with the liveliness of a Lola Montez. But to Lyman that romantic history is worthless. He says: "Every fourth-rate antiquarian in the West has panned Lola's poor gravel. My grandparents are a deep vein that has never been dug. They were *people*" (22).

It would be a mistake to consider Lyman merely the mouthpiece of Wallace Stegner. Yet much of what Lyman speaks for, Stegner expressed on other occasions. He shared Lyman's distaste for some of the student radicalism of the 1960s. Looking back on the decade of the 1960s in 1972, Stegner remarked that the student movement "started at Berkeley and we inherited it at Stanford [where Stegner taught]. The kids didn't come to learn, they came angry and with answers—not questions." He added: "I don't know why when you get mad at Mr. Smith, you break Mr. Jones's windows." Part of the problem, Stegner continued, was that we know so little about the past. "We have to keep our ties with the past to learn and grow," he told a reporter. "Cut loose from the past and we become nothing."12

Shortly before he wrote *Angle of Repose,* Stegner explained his purposes in the novel. "What I would really like to see some western writer manage to do," he related to English Professor John R. Milton, is "to put together his past and present." Then, turning to *Angle of Repose,* Stegner said he was writing a novel in which "some pretty refined *eastern* characters . . . are going to have some of the refinement ground out of them." Willa Cather had earlier argued that the frontier broke "the really refined." True, but Stegner added, "for people who weren't broken by it, . . . it could be a coarsening experience but also a strengthening one. So I've got some genteel-tradition folks who are going to have to develop a few calluses."13

In several ways, then, Stegner broke from earlier western stories. First of all, he gave a new twist to newcomers' experiences in the West. Rather than emphasizing change, he spoke of continuities, of replication. Scratch a westerner deeply enough, and one will find an easterner, like Susan Burling Ward, who has carried along much of her eastern cultural baggage and is forced to readjust her thinking and living to fit a new environment. The westerner is not something entirely new; if like Susan, the westerner may be as much a reluctant easterner as a new westerner.

Second, Stegner hints that if one wishes to understand the modern West he must also know the nineteenth century. The Gold Rush, labor disputes in the mines, and class conflicts in the camps and small frontier towns help one to comprehend Lyman Ward in the 1960s, as those occurrences helped to explain his grandparents nearly a century earlier. Lyman Ward seems to learn that the American West is the product of two angles of repose: between the East *and* West, and between the frontier *and* the Berkeley generation.

How much Stegner's *Angle of Repose* differed from other western storytellers becomes clear in comparison with the novels of Louis L'Amour. In nearly all of his novels, L'Amour limited his West to the years of first contact or early settlement. On occasion L'Amour dealt with East-West linkages, but most often his frontier men and families are depicted as innovators, as agents of change, not as carriers of eastern sociocultural attitudes, as Stegner depicts Susan and

Oliver Ward in *Angle of Repose*. Nor was L'Amour much intrigued with comparing western experiences over a century of time as Stegner had in his novel. Although they were contemporaries, L'Amour looked back to and followed the western story tradition emerging from Buffalo Bill, Owen Wister, Zane Grey, and dozens of other purveyors of popular western fiction. On the other hand, Stegner, building on the regional tradition of cultural developments in the West, was more interested in tracing continuities and changes over time within the region, from the frontier period to the present. Although Stegner frequently championed his more inclusive, complex form of western storytelling, he realized he had lost the popularity contest to L'Amour. When I asked Stegner the chief differences between himself and L'Amour, he replied with a chuckle, "Oh, a few million dollars."[14]

Stegner was not without his detractors. Some scholars accused him of misusing the life and letters of Mary Hallock Foote, failing to credit her as the major source for his novel. It was a charge that "irked" Stegner because, he said, he was writing a novel, not a biography. Besides, he added, he had cleared his work with Foote's descendants.[15] A leading Native American scholar also scored Stegner for, she charged, overlooking Indian history in all his major writings.[16] Still other readers thought Stegner much too critical of the countercultural impulses of the 1960s. Stegner never said much to his critics, although he frequently admitted that he wrote out of his own experiences. Other writers would have to tell different kinds of stories drawing on events, ideas, and peoples that he had not encountered.

For most readers and reviewers, however, *Angle of Repose* was a brilliant success. It not only illustrated Stegner's first-rank attributes as a skillful narrator, it also demonstrated his talents at characterization. Utilizing Susan Burling Ward as his major protagonist, Stegner abandoned the male-dominated plots of earlier western stories. In addition, seeing much of the world through Lyman Ward, the alienated and disillusioned narrator of the 1960s, allowed Stegner to add valuable complexities and ambiguities to his work.[17] Conducting an open marriage of history and fiction, Stegner addressed the central question of a probing western storyteller: what were the major influences that shaped the American West in its march from the frontier to its modern era? Few other western writers aimed as high, and none since Willa Cather and John Steinbeck achieved as much as Wallace Stegner in *Angle of Repose*.

THE PUBLICATION of Patricia Nelson Limerick's *The Legacy of Conquest: The Unbroken Past of the American West* (1987) stirred up more controversy than any other work of western history since Walter Prescott Webb's *Great Plains* in 1931. Although not the first shot of a historiographical civil war, Limerick's lively and smoothly written synthesis crystallized many of the interpretive conflicts arising since the 1960s. Historians championing new, revisionistic views of the western past praise Limerick's accomplishments, whereas dissenters harpoon the book as containing little new information and as too glib and popular in approach. Whatever one concludes about *The Legacy of Conquest*—and the reactions have often been partisan, emotional, and sometimes pointedly acrimonious—most readers will agree that it has attracted more attention than any book about the West since Henry Nash Smith's *Virgin Land: The American West as Symbol and Myth* (1950). While *Legacy* clearly illustrated several increasingly popular trends in post-1960s western historiography, it likewise demonstrated how this new story would break from the frontier historical narratives from Turner's time until the mid-twentieth century.[18]

The Legacy of Conquest appeared in the midst of yeasty times for western historians. For nearly a generation westerners had chipped away at much of the historiographical edifice erected during the first half of the twentieth century. The sociocultural eruptions of the late 1960s and early 1970s seemed to encourage this revisionism. Indeed, by the early 1980s, one could speak of a reorientation at work in several subfields of writing about the American West.

These transformations particularly influenced historical writings about ethnic, gender, and environmental topics. Well-known military historians like Francis Paul Prucha and Robert Utley, through their important works on Indian-white relations, paved the way for other revealing new studies of Indian history. Meanwhile, ethnic scholars such as Juan Gómez-Quiñones, Richard Griswold del Castillo, Albert Camarillo, and Nell Irwin Painter began to publish essays and books challenging earlier accounts overlooking the roles of Chicanos and African Americans in the history of the West. At the same time feminist historians Julie Roy Jeffrey, Sandra Myres, and Glenda Riley provided pioneering monographs and syntheses of women's experiences on the western frontier. Concurrently, Donald Worster, Richard White, and William Cronon opened the field of frontier and western environmental history through a handful of important books in that new field.[19]

Despite the pathbreaking publications in these and other areas of western history, no one had published a one-volume history of the West that drew on this innovative new research and supplanted earlier interpretations of the region. In 1987, Limerick's *Legacy of Conquest* did just that. Not only was her lively book a synthesis of the new scholarship, it told a story at odds with most of the historiographical narratives of the pre-1960s period. As had the writings of Frederick Jackson Turner, Walter Prescott Webb, Henry Nash Smith, and Earl Pomeroy, Limerick's notable volume broke from previous interpretations and provided a new story for those interested in the history of the American West. In addition, in content and tone *The Legacy of Conquest* paralleled changes at work in contemporary fiction and films about the West.[20]

In several ways, the life and career of Patricia Nelson Limerick illustrate major emphases in recent historical writings about the West. Reared in the town of Banning in southern California in a multicultural setting, Limerick made the requisite stops for a revisionist: breakfast in southern California, lunch at the University of California, Santa Cruz, dinner at Yale and Harvard, and after-dinner refreshments in Boulder. After early training in broader historical subjects, Limerick turned to American Studies and the American West at Yale, where she studied with noted western historian Howard Lamar. Following the completion of her doctorate, Limerick taught at Harvard and further honed her lively writing style as a Nieman Fellow.

While at Harvard, Limerick won a fellowship at the Charles Warren Center (1983–84) to read and write about the West. A year later her revised Yale dissertation *Desert Passages: Encounters with the American Deserts* (1985) was published, a clear indication of Limerick's strong interest in people-environmental relationships. Meanwhile, she began work on her most important work, an overview synthesis of western history based on recent writings about the West and influenced as well by Limerick's pilgrimage stopovers in California, at Santa Cruz, at Yale and at Harvard, and at the University of Colorado. These academic and personal experiences helped shape Limerick's *The Legacy of Conquest,* her most important work to date and the benchmark volume of the New Western history.[21]

In the opening and closing chapters of her provocative book, Limerick advances the central doctrines of the New Western history even as she points to the large limitations of the frontier or Turner thesis. Western historical writing suffers, Limerick boldly insists, from premature departures, from misplaced allegiances, and from blind avoidance of reality. Equally troubling, she adds, too many western historians overlook the complexities of the past, instead cheerfully and sometimes blindly following outmoded and even dangerous views of

Patricia Nelson Limerick

Patricia Nelson Limerick is often cited as the leading advocate of the New Western history. (Courtesy Patricia Nelson Limerick)

the West. Taken together, these outspoken criticisms suggest that Limerick had taken the offensive, a one-woman attack on much of the traditional story of western history.

First of all, as Limerick asserts in the subtitle of her book, an "unbroken past" links earlier and recent Wests. "When Western historians yielded to a preoccupation with the frontier and its supposed end," Limerick argues, "past and present fell apart, divided by the watershed of 1890" (18). Such amputated thinking about western history led westerners astray; they were unable to recognize how the issues of the pioneer West remained problems for the modern West. For example, the mistreatment of minority groups, the lust for profits, and the despoiling of nature continued to be dilemmas for the 1980s as they were for the mid-nineteenth century. These legacies of conquest remained much in evidence toward the end of the twentieth century.

For Limerick, westerners were blind to the molding power of continuity because of their excessive ties to frontier myth. Although the patriarch of frontier thinking, Frederick Jackson Turner, had moved on to postfrontier topics, historians still followed the frontier thesis. Turner and his hypothesis were, Limerick opined, "to put it mildly, ethnocentric and nationalistic" (21). Writers and readers who marched lockstep after the frontier ideology missed the vital connections that linked the nineteenth and twentieth centuries.

But, Limerick quickly added, important changes had occurred since the 1960s. Historians were now focusing on minority experiences *in* the West, as well as on other "particular Western places, people, and events." These new topics, and the studies based on them, had raised a "central irony: the very vitality of Western research, by exploding the model [of the frontier thesis], made mainstream historians declare that the field was dead." Then, in one of the most arresting of several rich metaphors in *Legacy of Conquest,* Limerick concluded "the breakdown of the old organizing idea fostered chaos; the corral built to contain Western history had been knocked apart" (22).

In place of the story of the American West as an expanding frontier, Limerick called for a narrative emphasizing conquest, over time, within the trans-Mississippi West. Hers was a regional West, an area in which contact, competition, conflict, and conquest were persisting themes. Viewing the frontier as Turner's meeting place between "savagery" and "civilization" and accepting the idea of a closing frontier in 1890s—these were false notions that must be dropped. In exchange were acceptance of a West with a continuous, unbroken history, especially one characterized by ethnic complexity, de-

The Legacy
of Conquest
THE UNBROKEN PAST OF
THE AMERICAN WEST

Patricia Nelson Limerick

The Legacy of Conquest (1987)

    The Legacy of Conquest (1987) provided a new gray story of the western past. Patricia Nelson Limerick's book frontally challenged the older frontier thesis of Frederick Jackson Turner. (W. W. Norton & Company, New York; jacket design Mike McIver)

structive capitalism, and environmental destruction. As Limerick put it succinctly, "Deemphasize the frontier and its supposed end, conceive of the West as a place and not a process, and Western American history has a new look" (26–27).

The reorientation of western storytelling Limerick calls for in her "Introduction" becomes the structural and topical blueprint for her volume. Dividing her 350-page book into two major parts of five chapters each, the author centers on three major subjects: ethnic diversity and conflict; economic motivations and resulting difficulties; and environmental misuse. The first part, "The Conquerors," deals primarily with the nineteenth century, whereas the second part, "The Conquerors Meet Their Match," treats the modern West more extensively. But all the chapters, whether in the first or second sections, emphasize strong linkages and continuities between the pre- and post-1900 Wests.[22]

For Limerick, the conquerors began with distorted, if not false, motivations that skewed much of what they did in the early West. Convinced of the rightness of their invasions into the wilderness and driven by an excessive lust for land, the earliest Euroamerican settlers spilled pell-mell into the frontier West. Blinded by their self-righteous convictions that they were merely helping themselves and others, they were confused when Indians fought back, when exaggerations of promoters proved untrue, and when the federal government failed to carry out the settlers' expectations. They saw themselves as "innocent victims," Limerick writes, as they fell into a pattern of "denial and dependence." A "passion for profit" had driven pioneers westward, and they were upset when their efforts ran into so much opposition, when their fields failed or became weed-infested, or when competitors failed to accept and follow their agendas.

Earlier tales of heroic pioneer adventure, Limerick argues, tell too little of the difficulties and complexities of the early West. Taking refuge in these romantic stories, pioneers and modern westerners alike miss the truths of the nineteenth-century West. Take, for example, the missionary wife Narcissa Whitman. Driven by her evangelical conviction that Indians were heathens in need of God, she went west to midwife their conversions. But little turned out as she expected. As Limerick writes, Narcissa's "life in Oregon provides little support for the image of life in the West as free and adventurous, and romantic. Most of the time, she labored" (38). Dreams of saving needy, accepting Indians soured into discontent and descended into the nightmare of tragedy, with the Whitmans losing their lives at the hands of the Cayuse Indians in

1847. The failure and destruction of Narcissa Whitman's dream is but one instance of a more complex, realistic western past Patricia Nelson Limerick places
before her readers.[23]

The final chapter in part one, "The Meeting Ground of Past and Present,"
makes explicit the continuities Limerick traces between the nineteenth and
twentieth centuries. She points to three such connections: "the region's dependence on federal money, instability in business cycles, and inconsistent en-
forcement of laws"; in all these areas, she adds, "the twentieth-century West
bore a strong family resemblance to that theoretically dead past" (134–35). Ongoing problems with water supply and irrigation policies, the continuing "high
tech gold rush" to Silicon Valley and elsewhere, and the appearance of Claude
Nichols and other new western outlaws are, to Professor Limerick, clear evidences of the unbroken past of the American West.

Three of the five chapters in part two of *The Legacy of Conquest* discuss the
complex relationships between whites and minority groups in the West. Previous stories of Native Americans and Hispanics were partially misfocused, according to Limerick, because they overlooked the Indian side of western
experiences and tried to force Hispanics into the narrative of a closing frontier,
where it obviously did not fit. In addition, conflicting reservation, termination,
and paternalistic/self-determination policies of the twentieth century prove
that nineteenth-century dilemmas in dealing with Indians continue in the
1980s. Similarly, border confrontations, issues of bilingualism, and inequities
in workplaces convince Limerick that Anglo-Hispanic tensions remain unresolved. She sees parallel continuities in mistreatment of Asians and blacks and
in persisting negative attitudes of Gentiles toward the Mormons in the nineteenth and twentieth centuries. Ethnocentric attitudes, biases toward the
"other," have ruled the West.

Throughout *The Legacy of Conquest,* Professor Limerick measures the impact of westerners on lands and landscapes, but she also devotes a full chapter ("Mankind the Manager") to these environmental concerns. Limerick
opens this section with one of the longest pen portraits in her entire book, in
which she details the important role of Chief Forester Gifford Pinchot in fos-
tering conservation policies at the beginning of the twentieth century. Attempting to bring a rational approach to the wise use of natural resources,
Pinchot and his Progressive ally President Theodore Roosevelt were convinced
they could teach other Americans the correct uses of land, water, and forests.
But greed, the desire for inordinate profits, and the unwillingness to ask de-

manding questions about people-nature relationships torpedoed the best efforts of Pinchot and his wise-use descendants. Here again, the "legacy of conquest" usually added up to negative results.

In the final chapter entitled "The Burdens of Western American History," Limerick plays on the title of a well-known book about the American South by the distinguished historian C. Vann Woodward. Examining the ongoing complexities of Indian policies, border and bilingual decisions involving Hispanics, and continuing dilemmas concerning the Mormons, Limerick reiterates the major theme of her controversial book: the burdens of the western past continue to disrupt and shape the western present. The only way westerners will understand this unbreakable chain between the nineteenth and twentieth centuries, Limerick clearly asserts, is to continue exploring the "conflict, unintended consequences, and complexities in Western history" (324). These legacies of conflict are everywhere evident in the final chapter of Limerick's book.

Two other events greatly accelerated the momentum that *The Legacy of Conquest* gained in telling a new story of the American West. In the Fall of 1989, a pathbreaking conference entitled "Trails: Toward a New Western History" and the subsequent publication of the conference papers in a widely circulated volume dramatically announced the New Western history. When the present writer asked Professor Limerick for a definition of the new movement, she prepared a one-page manifesto summarizing the tenets of the movement.[24] These emphases were at the center of Limerick's *The Legacy of Conquest* and her other publications and presentations in the 1990s. The writings of the New Westerners would emphasize place (the West as region) rather than process (the West as a moving frontier). These new historians would particularly include stories of ethnic groups, of women and families, and of the environment. And these narratives would not shy away from the disappointments and disasters that marked much of the history of the West. For Professor Limerick, such stories would eschew the triumphalist tone of too much previous writing and inject a more realistic tone and spirit into historical works about the American West. Overall, the New Western history promised to be more probing, lively, and balanced.

A key participant in the Trails roundup in 1989 was historian Richard White. Two years later his lengthy, analytical overview of the West appeared as *"It's Your Misfortune and None of My Own": A New History of the American West* (1991).[25] Nearly three times as long as Limerick's *Legacy* and a thorough, interpretive overview of the nineteenth and twentieth centuries, White's important book became *the* synthesis and text for many scholars and teachers accepting the new story of the American West. Like Limerick, and other historians such as Donald Worster and William Cronon, White viewed the West as riven with ethnic and class conflict, environmental disasters, and other legacies of human and physical conquest. As he had in his earlier books, *The Roots of Dependency* (1983) and *The Middle Ground* (1991), White also cast his story in the widest of contexts, showing how regional, national, and global circumstances shaped attitudes and policies.[26] For Richard White and for Patricia Nelson Limerick the western past had to be told as a complex, polyphonic story; anything less than that oversimplified and distorted western history.

In less than five years, then, the New Western history had stormed on the scene. From the publication of Limerick's *Legacy of Conquest* in 1987, through the Trails conference in 1989, and on to the publication of Limerick et al., *Trails: Toward a New Western History* and White's *"It's Your Misfortune and None of My Own"* in 1991, readers and teachers of western history were treated to important books and essays calling for new ways of telling western historical stories. Although journalists reporting on these events and most reviewers of the publications reacted positively or at least guardedly so, others were much more negative, coming after the New Western historians as wrongheaded, ill-informed, or (worst of all) malicious guides to western history.

Sometimes critics of the new historical storytellers seemed like angry detectives stalking brazen criminals. One historian referred to the New Western history as the "youngest whore on the block,"[27] another calls the new views "glamorized fascistic, thought-control history,"[28] and still another asserts that the New Western history "stresses the settlement of the West as a negative experience for almost everyone involved."[29] Less outspoken critics point to the excessively anti-Turnerian views, a distorting presentism, and a preponderance of negativism as major limitations of the New Western history.[30]

Proponents of the revisionist view fired back. Limerick dismissed some of the criticism as "that idiocy" and asserted that she was the target of "a lot of weirdness that has very little to do with . . . history." White thought some of the attacks betrayed the "resentment" of competitors, and Donald Worster asserted that too many western historians were unwilling to deal with the "moral failures" in western history.[31] For nearly a decade, this historiographical war has enlivened newspaper accounts, provoked spirited scholarly debates, and heightened interest in the frontier and American West. Some traditional storytellers claim that most Americans still view the frontier West as a dramatic, inspiring tale. Conversely, New Western historians are convinced that failure and defeat must be central themes in any realistic, persuasive account of the western past. Whom should one believe, who's right and who's wrong?

For our purposes here, right or wrong are not the major focus. Other questions are paramount: Have Patricia Nelson Limerick and the other New Western historians furnished a new story of western history? If so, in what specific ways does this narrative break from previous histories of the West? Even the harshest critics of Limerick et al. seem to argue that the New Western history represents an innovative metanarrative, one much different from the frontier stories of Frederick Jackson Turner, Frederic Logan Paxson, and Ray Allen Billington. These critics and other less critical observers point to the increased emphases on minority groups, the environment, and the destructive power of capitalism as ingredients missing from pre-1960s accounts. Furthermore, the tone and mood of the new histories seems more pessimistic and gray. Yet, among younger scholars, especially, these views have found ready acceptance.[32] For these academics, the New Western history has become the accepted story of the American West. Also for general audiences, some of the revisionist perspectives, especially the more sympathetic treatment of ethnic groups, the more pronounced environmentalism, and the more pessimistic views of government and bureaucracies, have gained widespread approval.

On second glance, however, the emergence of the New Western history and its wide acceptance are not so remarkable. Parallel new perspectives invaded and captured much of the historical profession in the United States.[33] And, as we shall see, the themes and moods that dominated the New Western history also characterized much of the fiction written about the West since the 1960s. These novelists, minority and mainstream alike, likewise discovered and told stories about a new gray West.

THE publication of N. Scott Momaday's Pulitzer Prize-winning novel *House Made of Dawn* (1968) signaled a dramatic change in western storytelling. No westerner of minority heritage—Indian, Hispanic, African American, or Asian American—wrote a widely recognized novel before the 1960s. The nonfiction writings of Charles Eastman (Sioux) and Luther Standing Bear (Sioux) and D'Arcy McNickle's novel *The Surrounded* (1936) attracted modest attention, but not until the appearance of novels by Momaday (Kiowa/Cherokee), Leslie

Marmon Silko (Laguna Pueblo), and James Welch (Blackfoot/Gros Ventre) in the late 1960s and the 1970s could one speak of a coterie of emerging Indian novelists.[34]

Simultaneously, other minority fictional voices began to be heard. Tomás Rivera's "*. . . y no se lo tragó la tierra*" (1971) and Rudolfo Anaya's *Bless Me, Ultima* (1972), the latter the most significant Chicano novel, represented important fictional works by Mexican Americans. Within the next two decades Chinese American writers Maxine Hong Kingston (*Woman Warrior*, 1976) and Amy Tan (*The Joy Luck Club*, 1989) published major books about Asian American experiences on the West Coast. Later, works by Indian novelists Louise Erdrich, Linda Hogan, and Sherman Alexie, Chicano writers Sandra Cisneros and Denise Chávez, and African American author Ishmael Reed proved that new, complex, multiethnic stories were beginning to emerge in the modern American West.

What was the special significance of these ethnic stories? In what specific ways did they challenge the traditional western narrative? Have these writers so successfully contested the Owen Wister-to-Louis L'Amour plotline, as some critics have argued, that the western story can never be told again in that way? Finally, are there any parallels in tone and perspective to be discovered between these ethnic writers and the New Western historians and a recent novelist like Larry McMurtry?

Selecting one novel to illustrate the importance of these new ethnic stories is a risky business. Nonetheless, Leslie Marmon Silko's *Ceremony* (1977) clearly suggests several of the notable features of the ethnic story.[35] In addition to providing a counterplot, an experimental style, and a contrasting perspective on white-Indian relations, the novel exudes comment on the nature of story and its meaning to a non-Anglo culture. On the other hand, Silko's novel need not be expected to carry all the multiple meanings of the ethnic story since it is, of course, an important individual work of literature in itself.

Leslie Silko's life is reflected in her fiction. Born of mixed heritage in the Laguna Pueblo of New Mexico, she was educated in Indian schools there, in a Catholic school in Albuquerque, and at the University of New Mexico. After graduating with highest honors in English, she began the study of law and then moved to writing. She taught briefly at Navajo Community College, lived in Alaska for two years, and next began her career as a professor of English at the University of Arizona in 1978. The recipient of a prestigious MacArthur fellowship, she has published, in addition to *Ceremony*, a small body of poetry and short fiction, a sampling of her work in *Storyteller* (1981), and a long novel *Almanac of the Dead* (1991), on which she worked for nearly ten years. For most of the last two decades Silko has lived in Tucson but also has continued to nourish her Native roots with many visits to New Mexico.[36]

It is for her major novel *Ceremony* that Silko deserves to be known. As Momaday had in his novel *House of Dawn,* Silko structures her story around a veteran, psychologically and emotionally maimed from his experiences in World War II. Like his creator, Tayo is a mixed-blood Laguna. More than that, his mother bore him out of wedlock, the son of a casual relationship with a white man. Then she abandons Tayo to his Auntie, where he grows up among his relatives: his maternal grandmother, Auntie and her husband Robert and their son Rocky, and his Uncle Josiah. Caught between the swirling and conflicting backgrounds of these family members and uncertain about his own her-

Leslie Marmon Silko

Leslie Marmon Silko, a Native American writer from New Mexico, told a complex story of psychological terror and healing in her novel *Ceremony* (1977). (Copyright Douglas Kent Hall)

itage, he joins the service, on the spur of the moment, with his cousin Rocky. During the horrendous conflicts in the Pacific, Tayo descends into hellish turmoil. The death of Rocky, whom Tayo had promised to return safely to his Pueblo family, pushes Tayo over the edge. He returns to the West Coast traumatized by his war experiences, his guilt at not staying home to help his family, and his persisting uncertainties about his own heritage.

Silko begins Tayo's story at this point. But that narrative moves in directions at odds with most stories of the West. It also follows an innovative format. As we shall see, in several ways, *Ceremony* represents the tradition-breaking western stories that began to appear in the late 1960s and afterwards.

The opening pages of Silko's novel reveal the unusual ways she will use story and stories. Beginning with a series of verses, the author tells of Thought-Woman:

> She is sitting in her room
> thinking of a story now
>
> I'm telling you the story
> she is thinking.
>
> Ceremony
>
> I will tell you something about stories,
> [he said]
> They aren't just entertainment.
> Don't be fooled.
> They are all we have, you see,
> all we have to fight off
> illness and death.
>
> You don't have anything
> if you don't have the stories.
>
> (1–2)

Uniting theme and form in these initial pages, Silko indicates the powerful, molding, and medicinal purposes of her story. "Story" becomes ceremonial, restorative, and a form of salvation for Tayo as he works his way toward healing. But the narrative of his transformation is not structured in a linear, straightforward plot. Instead, Silko uses numerous stories, syncopating present and past, to get at the historical and contemporary pressures leading to

Chapter Four

Tayo's illness. Like Momaday in *House of Dawn,* Silko resembles modernists such as James Joyce and William Faulkner in utilizing stream of consciousness and abrupt time shifts to suggest the complexity of sociocultural influences on characters.

The use of story in *Ceremony* is innovative in still another way. For nearly a century after Buffalo Bill's Wild West, white authors (usually male) viewed the West through the eyes of Europeans or Anglo Americans. These stories, often leading from contact to conflict, cast Native Americans in the position of the Other, the opponent. Only a few novels like Oliver La Farge's Pulitzer Prize-winning novel *Laughing Boy* (1929) and Frank Waters's *The Man Who Killed the Deer* (1942) attempted to view events through the eyes of Indian protagonists. Silko's *Ceremony* illustrates the flood of new novels, by non-Indians and Indians alike, that appeared after the 1960s and that told their stories from the viewpoint of Native Americans.[37]

Silko's *Ceremony,* although a revealing work reflective of Pueblo Indian culture and lore, avoids much of the angry, anti-white tone that characterized many works published by Native American authors after 1970. In fact, Silko's novel focuses almost as much on the destructive elements among the Pueblos as on white racism toward Indians. In the opening sections of *Ceremony,* Tayo is so overcome with insecurities about his mixed-blood heritage, his failures to protect his cousin Rocky and his Uncle Josiah, and his wrenching war experiences that he is sick unto death. True, he has to shake off negative white attitudes toward Indians and relearn lessons in Anglo schools that devalued his Native American heritage. Even more arduous are the lessons he must learn in avoiding "the destroyers," the forces of evil and "witchery" that lead him toward drunkenness, despair, and self-destruction. As Ts'eh, a mixed-race and supportive woman he meets in the mountains, tells him, he must avoid the destroyers because they want to end his restorative story toward wholeness. Instead, she says, "they want to change it. They want it to end here, the way all their stories end, encircling slowly to choke the life away. . . . They would end this story right here, with you fighting to your death alone in these hills" (231–32). Silko makes clear through this spokeswoman that some of the most vicious and destructive of Tayo's opponents are those of his own race.

Tayo comes to realize that his successful journey must not veer toward isolating individualism but toward a unifying sense of community. As Native American novelist and critic Louis Owens points out, "Tayo's individual identity disappears as he journeys toward the communal identity ultimately pro-

SIGNET•451-J8017•$1.95

LESLIE MARMON SILKO

CEREMONY

A YOUNG AMERICAN INDIAN'S SEARCH
FOR A MEANING TO HIS LIFE LEADS
HIM BACK TO HIS PAST TRADITIONS....
"A SPLENDID, VIVID, DRAMATIC
NOVEL—NOTHING IS LEFT OUT."
—THE NEW YORK TIMES BOOK REVIEW

Ceremony (1977)

    Ceremony (1977) illustrates the new ethnic stories that appeared with
increasing frequency after the 1960s. (Signet Book, New American Library)

nounced [at the end of the novel] by the pueblo elders within the kiva—the center of their world."[38] In addition to embracing the wholistic sense of discerning Natives, Tayo gradually learns to avoid those actions, institutions, and systems that would lead him down a separate, destructive path. The evil influences of the destroyers are to be shunned, although Tayo succumbs to them on two or three occasions. As the narrator tell us, Christianity was also divisive; it had "separated the people from themselves; it tried to crush the single clan name, encouraging each person to stand alone, because Jesus Christ would save only the individual soul; Jesus Christ was not like the Mother who loved and cared for them as her children, as her family" (68).

Instead of following such isolationist tendencies, Tayo gradually perceives that he must recommit himself to the ties that bind. After he begins the ceremony journey the medicine man Betonie outlines for him, Tayo returns to the mountains. There, awakening on a clear, cold morning, he experiences a moment of epiphany: "He took a deep breath of cold mountain air: there were no boundaries; the world below and the sand paintings inside became the same that night" (145). That illuminating experience, one scholar argues, shows Tayo that he is part of the larger Pueblo community but of even "another, greater community, of a set of constructive and destructive forces, and that in order to achieve wholeness, he has to accept the fact that things are complex and not static."[39] That is exactly the lesson Silko has Betonie teach Tayo. Like the grandfather in John Steinbeck's classic short story "The Leader of the People," Tayo begins to perceive how much he's a part of a world human community.

The key to this learning process is Tayo's relationship with Betonie, the medicine man. Despite his early reservations about the Navajo healer—the inside of his hogan resembles a dirty, unorganized junkpile and is located too close to the hellish portions of Gallup, New Mexico—Tayo comes to believe in and adopt the "story" Betonie tells him. Realizing that the medicine man's heritage is as complex and doubtful as his own and sensing the wisdom of Betonie's observations, Tayo begins his journey. Betonie shows Tayo that his story is part of much longer and complex stories, that they continually change and remain unfinished. When Betonie revealingly tells Tayo to "remember these stars," that he Betonie has "seen them," and the lost spotted cattle of Josiah, "a mountain," and "a woman," Tayo tries to pay for Betonie's evident wisdom. But Betonie refuses and says the ceremony (story) "has been going on for a long long time now. It's up to you," Betonie tells Tayo, "Don't let them stop you. Don't let them finish off this world" (152).

Once Tayo has discovered the recipe for the needed story or ceremony, Silko sends him to the mountains for his cleansing ordeal. Similar to several of Ernest Hemingway's heroes, Tayo abandons the lowlands or plains of jealousy, materialism, drunkenness, and self-doubts and goes to the pristine, restorative mountains to find himself. And he does—just as Betonie predicted. As Alan R. Velie notes, Tayo's search in *Ceremony* becomes "a Laguna Grail Story," even though Silko was unacquainted with the grail legend when she wrote the novel.[40] In the highlands, Tayo escapes, not without bruises and near failures, including several doubts and nightmares that beset him.

In one pregnant symbolic scene Silko catches much of the import of Tayo's quest in the mountains. In doing so, she unites the searcher and that for which he searches. Finding his Uncle Josiah's stolen cattle fenced in by greedy Texans (popular villains among most New Mexico writers), Tayo cuts the fence, allowing the cattle to escape and find their way back, eventually, to safety and satisfaction. Tayo follows the same pattern in his own quest. He metaphorically cuts the wires that fence him in, leaves behind most of the events and bad dreams that ensnare him, and runs toward a new understanding of himself and his larger world. The stars, the cattle, the mountains, and the woman that Betonie had foreseen become important stimuli for the new story Tayo will begin to live.

In the closing scenes of the novel, Tayo's experiences illustrate and clarify the story Betonie set before him. When Ts'eh, the woman in the mountains to whom Tayo has made love and whom he has come to love, warns him that the destroyers are coming after him, he leaves the mountains. Now, his newfound strength will be tested in the threatening lowlands. He nearly falters when the drunken Indian veterans, one example of the destroying forces, turn upon one another in a violent orgy, near a uranium mine where white engineers and miners have desecrated Pueblo lands. Tayo survives that temptation and returns to his pueblo to tell his story to the elders gathered in a kiva. When Tayo's Old Grandma, sitting by the stove as she does throughout the novel, hears some of these details and of other horrendous recent events, she says in the final sentence of prose: "It seems like I already heard these stories before . . . only thing is, the names sound different" (260). Indeed she has, and indeed they are.

When *Ceremony* appeared in 1977, Silko was quoted on the dustjacket as saying the novel dealt with "the powers inherent in the process of storytelling." Such stories, she added, had always been important Pueblo prescriptions for tribal maladies. Although her book dealt with one Native family, it had a much larger purpose: "the search for a ceremony to deal with despair, the most virulent of all diseases."[41] Or, as she told another author friend, "I believe more than ever that it is in sharing the stories of our grief that we somehow can make sense out—no, not make sense out of these things. . . . But through stories from each other we can feel that we are not alone, that we are not the first and the last to confront losses such as these." As healing medicine, her novel could work as stories in the Laguna Pueblo did, providing a sense of "community knowledge and concern" for anyone who had "suffered losses."[42]

In this psychological use of storytelling, as well as in several other ways, Leslie Silko's *Ceremony* was a new kind of western story. Like other western fiction about ethnic groups, her novel reversed the lens of the traditional western narrative. Ethnic figures became the heroes and heroines, and with Anglos sometimes now becoming the villains. But *Ceremony* is more than an anti-white tract; unlike the movie *Dances with Wolves* (1990), it does more than reverse the white hats and black hats. More importantly, ethnic novels like *Ceremony* portrayed the West through non-Anglo experiences, thereby furnishing a counter-narrative to *The Virginian* plot and broadening the meaning of the American West.

Moreover, *Ceremony* abandons the earlier emphasis on the lone individual as *the* western hero. Granted, Tayo sets out on a journey for self-knowledge, but what he comes to understand is the interconnectedness of all humans and their close links to the land and animals with which they exist. Silko communicates this theme of community and multilayeredness through a variety of means. Several of the major characters, including Tayo and Betonie, learn to accept their mixed-race backgrounds. They come to understand these heritages need not be conflictual, they may be mutually beneficial. In the closing pages of the novel, Tayo seems to represent the author's perspective when he cries after "finally seeing the pattern, the way all the stories fit together—the old stories, the war stories, their stories—to become the story that was still being told." Now, he saw the world as it truly was: "no boundaries, only transitions through all distances and time" (246).

Silko's experimental design in *Ceremony*, reinforcing her theme of the necessity of understanding and accepting multiple viewpoints, represented another clear break from the format of most previous western stories. Her nontraditional organization is most obvious in her nonlinear plot. The long-ago past, the immediate past, and the present cycle in and out of focus to add complexity and thick description to Tayo's search and to the lives and actions of the other characters who influence him. In addition, poetry and prose, straightforward and stream-of-consciousness narrative, repeatedly conflated throughout the novel, illustrate another narrative ingredient in Silko's novel. In form, as much as in idea, the author abandoned the architecture of earlier western tales.

Finally, like Wallace Stegner in *Angle of Repose,* Silko proves especially skilled in gender representations. Her portraits of the male figures, Tayo, Betonie, and Uncle Josiah, are particularly appealing; but so are her characterizations of Tayo's Auntie and old Grandma. Even the very brief vignette of Tayo's dissolute mother adds noticeably to the novel's strengths. Equally important is what Native American scholar Paula Gunn Allen terms the "feminine landscape" of *Ceremony.* In characterizing the land as feminine and in tying Spider Woman and Ts'eh to this "womanness," this "universal feminine principle of creation," Silko shows that Tayo's "initiation into womanhood is complete" when his story, his ceremony, reunites him with the land.[43]

Silko's *Ceremony* is an especially apt example of the new kinds of western stories appearing since the 1960s. Recentering the traditional story, Silko transforms it from a lone white male narrative into an ethnic communal story. She also gives the concept of "story" a much more complex and powerful meaning. Likewise, the intricate design of her novel clearly breaks from the linear, more traditional plots of most western stories. And, more than most New Western historians and recent western films, *Ceremony* contains an appealing, provocative portrait of gender relations in Leslie Silko's New West.

WHEN Larry McMurtry's mammoth novel *Lonesome Dove* appeared in 1985, it immediately gained widespread positive attention. The next year the novel received the Pulitzer Prize for fiction and in 1989 became the subject of an extremely popular, four-part television miniseries. The runaway best-selling book not only resuscitated McMurtry's floundered career, it also revealingly illustrated shifting popular attitudes about the American West during the late twentieth century. More than any other recent western novelist, Larry McMurtry, in *Lonesome Dove* and in such other works as *Anything for Billy* (1988) and *Buffalo Girls* (1990), depicted the new gray West that dominates much recent western storytelling.[44] If Wallace Stegner represented post-1960s writers who produced realistic regional fiction, if Patricia Nelson Limerick stands for a new crop of historians calling for probing and less romantic historiography, and if Leslie Marmon Silko speaks for a host of authors treating ethnic topics from new perspectives, Larry McMurtry stands for an expanding group of novelists, other writers, artists, and film-makers who re-imagine the West as a complex, unromantic region rife with flawed characters, uncertain values, and dangerous myths. This newly remythologized West has become the predominant western story in the 1980s and 1990s with Larry McMurtry as its leading storyteller.

McMurtry's backgrounds illuminate his increasingly significant role in the invention of the new gray West. Born in Wichita Falls, Texas, in 1936, he grew up well aware of his heritage as a grandson and son of Texas cattlemen. He soon realized, too, that his life in Archer City and on a nearby ranch in north-central Texas embodied a number of conflicts. During the life of McMurtry's grandfather, he had seen the last of the great northward-moving cattle drives of the nineteenth century. Moving on to the grandfather's ranch, McMurtry's father gradually gave up ranching, with his wife, his son Larry, and three younger children spending more time in Archer City than on the ranch. In his boyhood and adolescent years, McMurtry heard stories of the glories of the cattle kingdom and cowboy life even as that life disappeared. Towns and cities were quickly replacing the romantic cowboy god of earlier generations. As McMurtry stated in a later lecture, he "formed [his] consciousness in the period when . . . one set of values and traditions were being strongly challenged by another set of values and traditions." He "grew up just . . . when rural and social traditions in Texas were really, for the first time, being seriously challenged by urban traditions."[45] As we shall see, this conflict between two ways of life, as well as several other parallel conflicts, is a key to understanding the ambiguous, ambivalent, shifting emphases in McMurtry's thinking and writing.

Early on, McMurtry turned to writing. As a student at Archer City High School he won honors as budding author. Then as an undergraduate at Rice University and at North Texas State College (University of North Texas), from which he graduated in 1958, and as a graduate student in English at Rice from 1958 to 1960, McMurtry wrote dozens of short stories, essays, and poems. Some of these he published in campus magazines, many he destroyed as not worthy of publication. Meanwhile, and signally important for McMurtry's notable career as a western storyteller, he was trying to sort out his attitudes and emotions about an Old and New Texas and how he might write about the conflicts between these times and experiences.

Larry McMurtry

Larry McMurtry's experiences in Texas as the state wavered between its
cowboy gods heritage and its urbanizing present helped shape his many notable
novels about Texas and modern America. (Photo by Diana Lynn Ossana;
courtesy Larry McMurtry)

McMurtry's treatment of these sociocultural conflicts and his ambiguous attitudes about these clashes are keys to his entire career but especially for understanding his first novels. Once McMurtry published his initial novel in 1961, he proved to be an indefatigable worker, often turning out five, double-spaced pages each day. In less than fifteen years, before he reached his fortieth birthday, McMurtry had become a well-known American writer. Between 1961 and 1975, he published six novels, four of which became movies, a collection of essays, and dozens of reviews and scattered shorter pieces. Nearly all these works deal, at least in part, with tensions between men and women nourished on past myths no longer sustainable in a rapidly changing and increasingly complex present.

McMurtry's important first novel, *Horseman, Pass By* (1961), revealingly illustrates several of the author's life-long emphases.[46] This brief, much-revised work centered on a young Texan Lonnie, caught between the old-fashioned, cowboy god values of his aging grandfather Homer, and the views of his much younger uncle Hud, whose amoral and flashy life alienates even as it fascinates the adolescent central figure. The author's sympathies obviously do not lie with the devilish Hud, but neither do they champion the grandfather's lifestyle, which offers little for Lonnie. Instead, in the final scene, the young man climbs aboard a truck leaving the cattle country and headed for a nearby city. Like so many of McMurtry's protagonists, Lonnie must abandon the myth-ridden past—in this case the cowboy/cattleman legend—and head out for a hazy future. Young Lonnie's physical and psychological journey is reflected in the novel's title as are other characters' similar searches for mobility in *Leaving Cheyenne* (1963) and *Moving On* (1970).

In these three novels, as well as in another novel *The Last Picture Show* (1966) and in an early collection of essays *In a Narrow Grave* (1968), McMurtry focused on the traumatic experiences Texans, fictional and historical, faced in the transitions between the nineteenth and twentieth centuries. Next, he dealt with agonies of urban, rootless Texans, especially in Houston, as they searched for meaning in what seemed to be a chaotic world. For many reviewers, *All My Friends Are Going to Be Strangers* (1972) and *Terms of Endearment* (1975) were lesser artistic achievements than the first novels. And other naysayers joined them in citing McMurtry's falling production and his increasingly unsatisfactory novels as clear signs that the Texas author was losing his touch. For these readers and reviewers *Somebody's Darling* (1978), *Cadillac Jack* (1982), and *The Desert Rose* (1983) deserved to be forgotten.

Then *Lonesome Dove* flashed upon the scene in 1985.[47] This gargantuan novel not only rescued McMurtry's faltering career, it revived interest in western fiction and film, said by many observers to be in a decadent state in the 1970s and early 1980s. Had McMurtry written only *Lonesome Dove*, his high ranking among western storytellers would still be secure.

Even though some readers recognize the clear achievement of McMurtry's premier novel, they mis-read *Lonesome Dove*. McMurtry's gigantic work is not so much antimyth as metamyth. It does not replace earlier Westerns but is a magnificent retelling of the western story through a complex, provocative re-weaving of many of the familiar ingredients of the narrative. In one of his provocative essays, McMurtry points out *the* major difference between his work and that of revisionists like Patricia Nelson Limerick and other New Western historians. Instead of trying to supplant an earlier Triumphalist West with a new realistic Failed West, as the revisionists want to do, McMurtry wishes to deal with "the winning of the West . . . [as] an act based on a dream of empire dreamed by people with very different mentalities and ambitions from those historians or Westerners who may now direct a critical eye, quite fairly, at the legacy of that same dream and that same act." Revisionists often fail to see the larger, more complex Old West because, adds McMurtry, "they so rarely do justice to the quality of imagination that constitutes part of the truth. They may be accurate about the experience, but they simplify or ignore the emotions and imaginings that impelled the Western settlers despite their experience."[48] To his large credit, McMurtry understands and dramatizes the West "as imagination" in the plot, characterizations, and setting of *Lonesome Dove*.

The origins of *Lonesome Dove* are particularly revealing. For two decades McMurtry had urged Texas writers to avoid clichéd, well-worn plots about the nineteenth-century frontier West, exhorting them instead to deal with post-frontier and especially urban Texas. Vowing that he himself would not fall victim to the departed glories of the cowboy kingdom or the trail drive, he nonetheless was irresistibly drawn to those topics. Beginning in the 1970s he worked on a screenplay entitled "Streets of Laredo" dealing with a trail drive and the end-of-the-West theme. It was intended for a blockbuster film starring the aging western gods of Hollywood, John Wayne, Jimmy Stewart, and Henry Fonda. Then, in 1979, despite what he had said earlier about the necessity of avoiding trite subjects of the frontier, he told an interviewer he was thinking about writing "a novel about nineteenth-century Texas, particularly a trail-driving novel, since . . . trail drives were an extremely crucial experience, odd in that the whole period of the trail drives was so extremely brief, and yet out of it grew such an extraordinarily potent myth."[49]

With more than eight hundred pages in which to work, McMurtry tells a long, complicated story. True, his narrative follows the familiar path of the trail drive novel that authors Andy Adams, Emerson Hough, Benjamin Capps, and Robert Flynn traveled earlier, but McMurtry's plot is much more complex, shot through with several subplots, and peopled with a full gamut of varied characters. McMurtry also takes his time starting the two thousand mile trip from the Mexican Border to the Montana range north of Miles City near the Canadian boundary. He devotes two hundred pages to descriptions of the hot, dry, boring setting of Lonesome Dove before the herd begins to lumber northward. At first, it seems the cattle will never cross the Red River and leave Texas. Once they move past that river, the pace of the plot speeds up, like a trail-savvy herd anxious to find the end of the trail. As the cattle move north, McMurtry's subplots proliferate, causing his novel's organization to resemble a tree seen from its bottom up. Characters from Arkansas, Nebraska, and outlying areas move down the author's narrative branches to meet or join the trail herd as it heads for Montana.

McMurtry's meandering plot is chock full of revealing incidents and anecdotes. As expected, the cowboys experience stampedes, treacherous river crossings, vicious storms, conflicts with other trail herds, and confrontations with bears, snakes, and runaway horses. Equally dramatic are the violent struggles with Indians, marauding renegades, and other troubling humans. Through these numerous episodes McMurtry introduces a plethora of details, characters, and settings that diversify, enrich, and authenticate his story. McMurtry's cattledrive novel obviously follows the same journey motif so evident in several of his earlier novels. The picaresque structure is clear in all these works.

But it is not the plot that matters most in *Lonesome Dove*. McMurtry's rich cast of lively characters, when seen alongside the more traditional figures of Zane Grey, Louis L'Amour, and those of many other contemporary western storytellers, demonstrate why the novel won a Pulitzer Prize and remains one of the most talked-about western stories of the past generation. The most important characters in McMurtry's novel, Woodrow Call and Augustus (Gus) McCrae, are former captains in the Texas Rangers, now merely existing in the sandy, bleak, isolated hamlet of Lonesome Dove. The taciturn, unromantic half of the duo, Call outrageously drives himself and his workers. As Gus says of his partner, "you never had no fun in your life. You wasn't made for fun. That's my department" (170). Call fears his emotions, wishes to forget that he sired

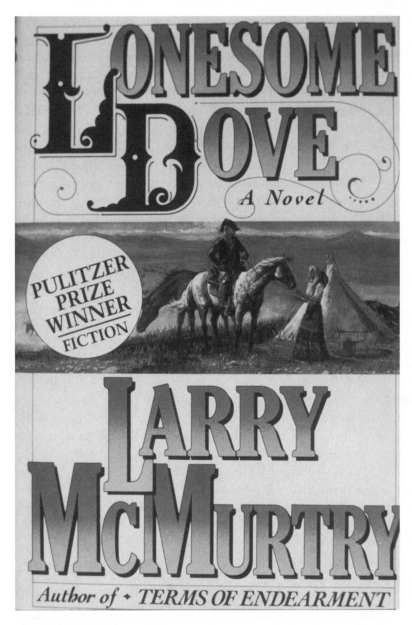

Lonesome Dove (1985)

More than any other recent novel, Larry McMurtry's *Lonesome Dove* (1985),
which won a Pulitzer Prize, represents the new gray story of the American West.
(Simon and Schuster, New York; jacket design George Corsillo)

a son through the young prostitute Maggie, and refuses to acknowledge his ties to other humans.

Conversely, Gus is a lazy, hard-drinking, loquacious, aging malcontent. He's also the conduit for most of the novel's humor. Harassing his partner Call, questioning the masculinity of the other riders, and frequently lauding his own sexual prowess, Gus talks and talks alongside the often silent Call. If the cook were to die, says Call on one occasion, they would have to put up with Gus. "In that case we'll have to eat talk, or else starve to death listening" (106). The narrator adds that "It was well known that Gus would talk to a stump if he couldn't find a human" (183). Providing comic relief in the novel, Gus also becomes, as we shall see, the mouthpiece for most of the statements about a closing frontier and wilderness-versus-settlement in the novel.

Several other men are among McMurtry's major characters. One of these is Jake Spoon, a former Ranger, but of much less stern stuff than Call or Gus. As the latter says of Jake, he "was always nervous. He's seen more Indians that turned out to be sage brushes than any man I know" (80). And when a young cowboy begins to idolize Jake, Gus muses: "he liked Jake, but felt him to be too leaky a vessel to hold so much hope" (157). Ironically, it's the deeply flawed Jake who talks Call into launching the trek to Montana. Two others, Deets, a black rider, and Newt, the unacknowledged son of Captain Call, are important members of McMurtry's human remuda. The only man who rivals Call's splendid energy and awesome skills, Deets is the cowboy on whom everyone depends. Modeled on Bose Ikard, cattleman Charlie Goodnight's marvelous black companion, Deets becomes, in McMurtry's novel, one of the most memorable African Americans in western fiction.[50] Meanwhile, Newt occupies a role in this novel similar to that of young Lonnie in *Horseman, Pass By*. He has to grow up under the traumatic pressures of the drive. By the end of the novel he has proven himself a worthy rider, even in the demanding eyes of his father. Repeatedly, McMurtry uses the aging Call and Gus and youthful Newt as varying viewpoints from which to examine happenings within the novel.

Lonesome Dove is a novel about men, it is a man's book. Yet two women play important roles, revealing much about frontiersmen's sexual attitudes and women's thoughts about themselves. Lorena Wood, a blond, beautiful, young whore, is the major female figure. Most of the cowboys love Lorena, though often equating ejaculation with genuine love. Driven into prostitution out of economic necessity after being abandoned by one of McMurtry's selfish, egocentric men, Lorena is forced to service the sexual appetites of Lonesome

Dove's male population even as she dreams of fleeing to San Francisco. Controlled and nearly destroyed in a patriarchal West, Lorena makes a bad choice by relying on the irresponsible Jake Spoon. She joins the cattle drive, only to be left unprotected by Jake and stolen away by the most vicious of the novel's villains, Blue Duck, who sells her to a gang of cutthroat outlaws and renegade Indians. Gang raped and near death, she is narrowly rescued by the courageous Gus. Slowly and gently, he nurses her back to health. Lorena relies on Gus, coming to think she loves him. In the final section of the novel, now on the road to recovery, she takes leave of the men to join the other major female character on a small, isolated Nebraska farm.

Although as many critics as cowboys seem in love with Lorena,[51] Clara Allen is the more remarkable figure. Memorable married women in western stories are as unusual as creditable ministers, making Allen all the more noteworthy. We learn much about Clara, through Gus's strong remembrances of her, even before she appears well into the second half of the novel. Gus wanted to marry Clara, but clear-eyed, spunky realist that she was (and is) she realizes that union would not have worked. As Clara told Gus before going off to marry a rather dull, naive horseman, "Two racehorses like us would never get along. I'd want to be in the lead, and so would you" (682). Gus's rich memories of her sassy ways are reason enough for him to go on the trail drive since the herd will pass close to her small farm/ranch near the Platte River in Nebraska.

Clara's abundant strengths, wit, and practicality sparkle in conversations with several other characters. As her husband lies upstairs dying from a serious injury, she takes over his horse wrangler work, keeps up with her domestic duties, and looks after several guests. A woman of emotion, Clara grieves the loss of children, especially her sons, but, unlike all the other women in the novel, she is realistic about a world in which failures and disappointments often outrun successes. To his credit, McMurtry makes Clara believable in every respect.

Clara plays an important role in another way. When Call returns through Nebraska with the body of Gus, which he plans to bury in Texas, Clara lashes out at him, her fury full of gender implications rarely evident in pre-1960s stories:

> And I'll tell you another thing: I'm sorry you and Gus McCrae ever met. All you two done was ruin one another, not to mention those close to you. Another reason I didn't marry him was because I didn't want to fight you for him every day of my life. You men and your promises: they're just excuses to do what you plan to do anyway, which is leave. You think you've always done

right—that's your ugly pride, Mr. Call. But you never did right and it would be a sad woman that needed anything from you. You're a vain coward, for all your fighting. I despised you then, for what you were, and I despise you now, for what you're doing. (831)

In covering such a large swatch of the physical West, McMurtry has ample space to introduce a panoply of other actors. For example, in this post-Custer setting, we hear about or encounter several bands of Native Americans. Although the famed southern plains raiders, the Comanches, seem now under control, other groups wander throughout the region north of Texas. Displaced and powerless, they are nearly always hungry. Some beg the drovers or settlers for food; others violently castrate or rape the non-Indians they encounter. Like most of the novel's characters, the Indians are gray, ambiguous figures, bereft of their earlier moorings, unable to adjust to the new invaders.

Similar kinds of people in *Lonesome Dove* exist precariously on farms or ranches or in small towns. Most of these residents also suffer from alienation, depression, or boredom. Whether staying for the moment in Lonesome Dove or San Antonio, in Wichita or Fort Smith, or in Ogallala or Miles City, or attempting to homestead or ranch, McMurtry's characters seem dissatisfied or unable to settle down. Their futures, like their present circumstances, are bleak and depressing. Their unrealistic dreams, similar to Lorena's longing for San Francisco or Gus's desires for Clara, often turn to disappointments—if not to nightmares.

Not all of the physical or psychological terrain in *Lonesome Dove,* however, is unremittingly adverse and discouraging. At the end of the drive, Montana looms like a New Eden, open to the ambitious and courageous men willing to take up the challenges of the open country, as the trailers see it. And the semi-settled farm/ranch where Clara lives serves as an oasis from the threatening physical and social landscapes and peoples that surround it. Just as the valiant Call and his men, including the newly matured Newt, can settle and control Montana, so the ambitious, hard-working and no-nonsense Clara can wrestle a living from the Nebraska plains. In McMurtry's West only the most courageous, realistic, and tireless workers can succeed, and not without many bruises, dashed hopes, and defeats mixed among their achievements.

Lonesome Dove also illustrates McMurtry's talents in providing what he called "texture" in his fiction. For McMurtry, action and outward characterization are less important than the emotional and mental landscapes of his characters. Equally salient for achieving the desired texture is a fluidity of time, from the past to present and even on to the future. As McMurtry wrote in the late 1960s, writers had "coped fairly well with the physical circumstances of life in Texas, but our emotional experience remains largely unexplored."[52] At the core of *Lonesome Dove* is the powerful revelation of the inward skies of its major characters. Via the omniscient narrator, as well as from the protagonists themselves, we begin to understand the reasons for their actions. Call's inability to accept his affair with Maggie helps illuminate his reluctance to acknowledge Newt as his son. Gus's failure in winning Clara aids in understanding his two flawed marriages, his early irresponsible attitudes toward Lorena, and his continual need to dominate women. Meanwhile, the early misuse and abuse Lorena receives from men casts light on her inability to find a satisfactory love relationship with men during the trail drive. The nurturing and individualistic backgrounds and experiences of Clara before the novel opens prepare the reader for her redeeming and sustaining actions in the second half of the work.

In displaying the emotional textures of his characters as well as in providing the *longue dureé* of their lives, McMurtry makes apt, abundant use of memory. When we hear of the numerous dramatic activities of Call and Gus as Texas Rangers in the previous generation or two of white settlement in Texas, we understand Call's need, like Ernest Hemingway's hero in *The Old Man and the Sea,* to go on another escapade to re-prove his courage and manhood. Although Call thinks "the old crew [of Rangers] was mostly a memory . . . [and life] was all changing" (487), his attitudes toward his work, women, and the journey northward are inextricably linked to those shaping memories. In the same way, even though Gus resembles a lazy, drunken, blabbermouth in the opening scenes, he quickly exhibits his nearly foolhardy bravery in heated contests with outlaws and Indians. Recalling his need for action, Gus tells Call, "I'd rather go outlaw than be a doctor or a lawyer" (726). And a few scenes later, Gus clarifies the long trajectory of his and Call's careers: "I can't think of nothing better than riding a fine horse into a new country," he tells Newt. "It's exactly what I was meant for, and Woodrow too" (744). Other such strong memories power and shape (sometimes *mis*shape) the lives of Lorena, Clara, Deets, Jake, and the devilish Blue Duck.

In his skillful use of history and memory, McMurtry explodes the meaning of time in his novel. By doing so, he greatly enlarges the significance of his story and breaks from the format of many previous Westerns. Consider, for example, how little we know about the life of the hero and the history of Wyoming before the action takes place in *The Virginian.* Even less is evident about the pasts of Zane Grey's and Louis L'Amour's heroes. And the previous life of Shane is as indistinct as his future. Truth to tell, most western stories focus on brief, dramatic moments of conflict. That means history is truncated, forced to take most of its meaning from condensed sequences of frenetic action or adventure. But McMurtry, as do Stegner in *Angle of Repose* and Silko in *Ceremony,* provides readers with a strong sense of passing time. Indeed, *Lonesome Dove* overflows with ideas, actions, and descriptions depicting a closing, or at least a quickly changing, frontier as well as the opening of a new Anglo settlement in Montana. McMurtry's story takes place in a specific time, but the story's meaning is magnified by the author's placing those events in a sweeping overview of a rapidly shifting West.

In still one other way McMurtry enlarges the significance of the western story. His broad-canvas settings, his varied characters, and his clever use of time, memory, and history allow McMurtry to comment on the central ingredients of the western myth. One of these mythic emphases is the cowboy god. The clear human limitations of persons like Call, Gus, and Jake—their mistreatment of women, their willingness to steal for their own benefit, their violence—undercut and tarnish their reputations as well as those of the mysterious man on horseback who rides through so many western narratives. Nor is the West they inhabit an edenic Valhalla. Rather, McMurtry's West is primarily a series of subregions suffering from undesirable climates, settings riven with violent discord, or places dark and boring. Although McMurtry employs familiar ingredients of the western story—cowboys, a cattle drive, and the frontier—he undercuts and remythologizes these subjects to create a new gray West.[53]

McMurtry's large and important achievements became clearer if less subtle in two of his next novels. *Anything for Billy* (1988) and *Buffalo Girls* (1990) are even more explicit examples of McMurtry's desire to reinvent a less romantic and myth-ridden West.[54] In his treatments of Billy the Kid, Calamity Jane, and Buffalo Bill Cody, McMurtry dissects the legends surrounding these frontier demigods. In his fiction they become violent, tearful naifs like Billy; crying, boozing hermaphrodites like Calamity; or phony, shallow showmen like Buffalo Bill. More than merely carrying out myth-destroying revisionism, however, these novels present a new complex western past. Merely to demolish western myths is to exchange one narrowness for a new one. Instead, by creating ambiguous characters embodying historical and fictional truths, McMurtry thickens his description of the western past. In these two later novels, as he had in *Lonesome Dove,* Larry McMurtry invents a new gray West.

Epilogue

Toward a New Gray Story

WESTERN NOVELIST Willa Cather once asserted that the world broke apart in 1922. For Cather, the 1920s marked a clear watershed between premodern and modern worlds. Had she been alive nearly a half-century later, Cather might have pointed to the 1960s and 1970s as a parallel but less abrupt dividing point in western storytelling. These recent transformations in stories about the West since the 1960s, in addition to reorienting the content and tone of narratives about the American West, also reveal a good deal about shifting cultural and social attitudes in recent America.[1]

Recall that stories about the West in the three decades immediately following the Civil War depicted a white male heroically confronting demanding physical landscapes and worthy human opponents. Buffalo Bill's Wild West, dime novel Westerns, and historian Frederick Jackson Turner celebrated a region ripe for possible entry and settlement. These representations of the frontier West stress, above all, the need for courageous men to serve as the outriders of expansion and civilization in the spread of America to the West Coast.

In focusing on white heroes who captured and refined the frontier, these Creations Stories, while speaking for Manifest Destiny, paid scant attention to the roles of women and minority groups. Early in the twentieth century, these Untold Stories of women and minority figures, rediscovered and newly appreciated in recent decades, were powerless to reshape stories about the West. The fiction and artwork of Mary Hallock Foote, the extraordinary pioneer life of Calamity Jane, the lifestory of Indian warrior Geronimo, and the fiction of mixed-blood Mourning Dove illustrate the counter-narratives unable to redirect the western story before the 1960s.

Meanwhile, the earlier Creation Stories gradually hardened into the Traditional Stories that dominated the first half of the twentieth century. From

Epilogue

Owen Wister's novel *The Virginian* through the dozens of Westerns by B. M. Bower, Zane Grey, and Ernest Haycox, and on to the enormously popular frontier novels of Louis L'Amour, hundreds of authors wrote western stories featuring bold, masculine heroes resembling John Wayne and Gary Cooper. These valiant men entered and settled a dangerous, demanding West. In the interwar decades biographers like Walter Noble Burns and classic films such as *Stagecoach* portrayed Billy the Kid, Pat Garrett, and Wayne's Ringo Kid in their lively stories. For these writers and film-makers, the Old West, though vanished, remained alive. By the middle of the twentieth century, the frontier, and the winning of it, struck most Americans as a powerful, emulative story well worth retelling.

The yeasty sociocultural changes that swept across the United States from the mid-1960s through the mid-1970s helped usher in new stories of the American past. The heightened national interest in racial/ethnic, gender, environmental subjects, not surprisingly, clearly influenced storytelling about the American West.

But these New Stories of the West did not spring like a full-bodied Athena from the head of a western Zeus. Well before the 1960s, others had dealt with some of these subjects. A few writers like Oliver La Farge and D'Arcy McNickle treated Native Americans in their fiction, Willa Cather and John Steinbeck pictured strong women in their novels, and Wallace Stegner and A. B. Guthrie, Jr., emphasized environmental themes. A host of regional writers, too, urged other western storytellers to avoid sensational yarns of a wild frontier and to deal instead with the West as a unique, developing society. Finally, before the 1970s, novelists H. L. Davis, Steinbeck, and Walter Van Tilburg Clark frequently depicted the West in far from triumphant tones, thereby prefiguring later portraits of the region as a gray place.

Still, the tumultuous events of the late 1960s and early 1970s greatly accelerated changing attitudes about the American West and helped engender revised stories of the region and its inhabitants. As we have seen, the New Stories that emerged thereafter told of a transformed West. Stegner's *Angle of Repose* gave readers enlarged understandings of East-West linkages, class differences, and families in the West. In the 1980s Patricia Limerick's *Legacy of Conquest* provided a more critical, much less optimistic view of the West, illustrating several tenets of the New Western history. Meanwhile, Leslie Marmon Silko's *Ceremony* represented the dozens of new novels, primarily by minority writers, that furnished fresh ethnic perspectives on the western past and present. For Texas novelist Larry McMurtry, the needed New Story was not so much the destruction of the mythic Old West but expanded, more complex portraits of it. His Pulitzer Prize-winning *Lonesome Dove* did just that, proving that New Stories need not be debunking or radical revisionist views of the past.

These, then, were the major transformations in the western story from the Civil War to the present. The shifts tell us much about changing views of the American West. If early on Cody, the dime novelists, and Turner celebrated a frontier of opportunity open to expansion, storytellers after the 1960s, with a few notable exceptions like Louis L'Amour, were less sanguine about the western past or present. Many novelists, historians, film-makers, and artists told New Stories about an emerging gray West.

These narratives depicting a deeply flawed West were not unique to the region, however. They echoed the sentiments of many other contemporary storytellers in the United States. The trends in western storytelling after the 1960s clearly followed national currents.

A second glance at these later trends suggests something even more complex than merely a transition from Traditional Stories to New Stories in the past generation. In a recent review, Richard White, widely considered our most erudite western historian, writes that "on the whole, Americans prefer cheerful history."[2] Undoubtedly true. But perhaps a slightly different observation is equally correct: Americans do not cherish gloomy history. Both of these propositions help one to understand another take on western stories.

Truth to tell, Americans want a variety of stories. Even while New Western historians like Limerick and White present less optimistic portraits of the past, the widely read works, for example, of historian and biographer Robert Utley, known for their strong, appealing narratives of the Old West, have swept well beyond the New Western histories in sales. Utley's biographies of Billy the Kid and Sitting Bull and his studies of Native Americans and mountain men have all been best-sellers. Even more astounding are the sales of Stephen E. Ambrose's *Undaunted Courage: Meriwether Lewis, Thomas Jefferson, and the Opening of the American West* (1996). Selling in the millions, Ambrose's realistic work presents an engrossing, dramatic Traditional Story: courageous and adventuresome white men advancing into a threatening wilderness where they encounter earlier frontier peoples.

The same sales imbalances are clear in the circulation figures of western journals dealing with the American West. Where the best-known scholarly journal in the field, *Western Historical Quarterly,* publishes about 2,500 copies of each issue and *California History* and *Montana: The Magazine of Western History* boast of circulations between 7,500 and 12,000, the *Wild West* magazine, touted as "chronicling the frontier," sells more than 150,000 copies bimonthly. In addition, the circulation figures of *Old West* and *True West*, purveyors of lively stories of the pioneer West, far outdistance those of their more academic competitors.

These contradictory trends—the rise of New Stories and yet the clear staying power of Traditional Stories—are delightfully illustrated in Larry McMurtry's universally popular *Lonesome Dove*. This sprawling novel marries revised views about race and ethnicity, gender relations, and the environment to the familiar plot of a trail drive novel. McMurtry moves beyond the contest of the Old and New Wests to provide a New Gray Story, an oxymoronic West combining elements from Traditional and New Stories. Judging from the enthusiastic responses of readers and viewers to the fictional and cinematic versions of *Lonesome Dove*, it may be *the* model for complex western stories of the future.

One conclusion, however, overshadows all others. For more than a century, Americans have told thousands of widely circulated stories about the trans-Mississippi West. Even though shifting sociocultural currents have prompted clear changes in the content and tone of these western stories, large interest in the American West and narratives about the region remains unabated. One can be certain that, with a new century before us, Americans, as well as those outside the United States, will continue to be fascinated with the American West. Western stories, Traditional and New, as well as combinations of the two, will be told well into the next millennium.

Notes

Prologue: Origins of the Western Story

1. Don Russell, *The Lives and Legends of Buffalo Bill* (Norman: University of Oklahoma Press, 1960).

2. Loren Baritz, "The Idea of the West," *American Historical Review* 66 (April 1961): 618–40. For a recent book-length study of the mythic West, especially its European backgrounds, see Jan Willem Schulte Nordholdt, *The Myth of the West: America as the Last Empire* (Grand Rapids, Mich.: Eerdmans, 1995).

3. Richard Slotkin, *Regeneration Through Violence: The Myth of the American Frontier, 1600–1860* (Middletown, Conn.: Wesleyan University Press, 1973).

4. Richard W. Etulain, *Re-imagining the Modern American West: A Century of Fiction, History, and Art* (Tucson: University of Arizona Press, 1996), xv–xxviii.

5. George Ward Nichols, "Wild Bill," *Harper's New Monthly Magazine* 34 (February 1867): 273–85.

Chapter One: Creation Stories

1. Unless otherwise noted, this section on Buffalo Bill Cody draws heavily on Don Russell's thorough biography *The Lives and Legends of Buffalo Bill* (Norman: University of Oklahoma Press, 1960).

2. Russell, *Buffalo Bill,* 179. Richard J. Walsh, *The Making of Buffalo Bill* (Indianapolis: Bobbs-Merrill, 1928).

3. Henry Blackman Sell and Victor Weybright, *Buffalo Bill and the Wild West* (New York: Oxford University Press, 1955); Craig F. Nieuwenhuyse, "Six Guns on the Stage: Buffalo Bill Cody's First Celebration of the Conquest of the American Frontier" (Ph.D. dissertation, University of California, Berkeley, 1981).

4. The Harold McCracken Library at the Buffalo Bill Historical Museum at Cody, Wyoming, houses an extensive collection of Cody scrapbooks, which include hundreds of newspaper reports about the annual Wild West shows. Other Buffalo Bill scrapbooks are housed at the Western History Collections in the Denver Public Library. Newspaper quotations are from John Burke (Richard O'Connor), *Buffalo Bill: The Noblest Whiteskin* (New York: G. P. Putnam's Sons, 1974), 99, 102. Louisia Frederici Cody (with Courtney Ryley Cooper), *Memories of Buffalo Bill* (New York: Appleton, 1919).

5. Joseph G. Rosa, *Wild Bill Hickok: The Man and His Myth* (Lawrence: University Press

of Kansas, 1996); Joseph G. Rosa and Robin May, *Buffalo Bill and His Wild West: A Pictorial Biography* (Lawrence: University Press of Kansas, 1989).

6. Russell, *Buffalo Bill*, 214–35.

7. Burke, *Buffalo Bill*, 120–26, 151 ff.

8. Jay Monaghan, *The Great Rascal: The Life and Adventures of Ned Buntline* (Boston: Little, Brown and Company, 1951).

9. Sell and Weybright, *Buffalo Bill and the Wild West*, 162. Paul L. Reddin, *Wild West Shows* (Urbana: University of Illinios Press, 1999).

10. Program for "The Wild West," in 1883, Don Russell Collection, Series I:G, Buffalo Bill's Wild West, Box 1, Folder 3, Buffalo Bill Historical Museum, Cody, Wyoming.

11. Nate Salsbury gives his account of the beginnings of the Wild West show in Salsbury, "The Origin of the Wild West Show," *Colorado Magazine* 32 (July 1955): 204–14.

12. Nellie Snyder Yost, *Buffalo Bill: His Family, Friends, Fame, Failures, and Fortunes* (Chicago: Swallow Press, 1979), 134.

13. Program for "The Wild West," 1883; Sara J. Blackstone, *Buckskins, Bullets, and Business: A History of Buffalo Bill's Wild West* (New York: Greenwood Press, 1986).

14. Joseph Schwartz, "The Wild West Show: 'Everything Genuine,'" *Journal of Popular Culture* 3 (Spring 1970): 656–66.

15. Salsbury, "Origin of the Wild West Show"; Don Russell, *The Wild West, or, a History of the Wild West Shows . . .* (Fort Worth, Texas: Amon Carter Museum, 1970), 8, 10.

16. *Boston Evening Transcript*, August 12, 1884, quoted in William E. Deahl, Jr., "A History of Buffalo Bill's Wild West Show, 1883–1913" (Ph.D. dissertation, Southern Illinois University, 1974), 26.

17. For the roles of Indians in Cody's Wild West, as well as those in several other similar performances, see the exhaustively researched and well-written study by L. G. Moses, *Wild West Shows and the Images of American Indians 1883–1933* (Albuquerque: University of New Mexico Press, 1996).

18. Glenda Riley, *The Life and Legacy of Annie Oakley* (Norman: University of Oklahoma Press, 1994); Official Program: *Buffalo Bill's Wild West* (Hartford, Conn.: Calhoun Printing Company, 1885).

19. Don Russell, *Buffalo Bill*, 322.

20. *New York Dramatic Mirror*, March 12, 1887, in Deahl, "Buffalo Bill's Wild West Show," 61.

21. Russell, *Buffalo Bill*, 335.

22. Russell, *The Wild West*, 42.

23. Schwartz, "'Everything Genuine.'"

24. Official program: *Buffalo Bill's Wild West and Congress of Rough Riders of the World* (Chicago: Blakely Printing Company, 1893).

25. Yost, *Buffalo Bill*, 238.

26. For an opposing view, one that emphasizes the changes Cody made in his story of the West, see Richard Slotkin, "The 'Wild West,'" *Buffalo Bill and the Wild West* (Brooklyn, N.Y.: Brooklyn Museum, 1981), 27–44.

27. Richard White, "Frederick Jackson Turner and Buffalo Bill," in James R. Grossman, ed., *The Frontier in American Culture* (Berkeley: University of California Press, 1994), 6–65.

28. Philip Durham, "Introduction," in Durham, ed., *Edward L. Ellis, Seth Jones and Edward L. Wheeler, Deadwood Dick on Deck* (Indianapolis: Bobbs-Merrill, 1966), v–xiv. The most recent anthology of dime novels includes a superb introduction and helpful editorial apparatus; see Bill Brown, ed., *Reading the West: An Anthology of Dime Novels* (Boston: Bedford Books, 1997).

29. Henry Nash Smith, *Virgin Land: The American West in Symbol and Myth* (Cambridge, Mass.: Harvard University Press, 1950), 92; Christine Bold, "Malaeska's Revenge; or, The Dime Novel Tradition in Popular Fiction," in Richard Aquila, ed., *Wanted Dead or Alive: The American West in Popular Culture* (Urbana: University of Illinois Press, 1996), 21–42; quote on 24–25.

30. Throughout this discussion on dime novel Westerns, I am much indebted to the best source on the subject: Daryl Jones, *The Dime Novel Western* (Bowling Green, Ohio: Bowling Green University Popular Press, 1978). See also the pioneering discussion of dime novel heroes and heroines in Smith, *Virgin Land,* 90–120.

31. Jones, *Dime Novel Western,* 42.

32. Russell provides a chapter-length discussion of the Buffalo Bill dime novels, as well as a list of the dime novels Cody wrote and those written about him, in *Buffalo Bill,* 386–415, 494–503. Kent Ladd Steckmesser, *The Western Hero in History and Legend* (Norman: University of Oklahoma Press, 1965). Smith, *Virgin Land,* 104.

33. Jones, *Dime Novel Western,* 67–68; Smith, *Virgin Land,* 105.

34. Russell, *Buffalo Bill,* 388–92.

35. Jones, *Dime Novel Western,* 67–73; Prentiss Ingraham, *Adventures of Buffalo Bill, from Boyhood to Manhood* (1881), reprinted in E. F. Bleiler, ed., *Eight Dime Novels* (New York: Dover Publications, 1974), 92.

36. The classic bibliographical study of the dime novel includes a discussion of Edward L. Wheeler and his Deadwood Dick series: Albert Johannsen, *The House of Beadle and Adams and Its Dime and Nickel Novels,* 2 vols. (Norman: University of Oklahoma Press, 1950; supplement 1962).

37. Edward L. Wheeler, *Deadwood Dick, The Prince of the Road; or, The Black Rider of the Black Hills* (1877; Cleveland, Ohio: Arthur Westbrook, Co., 1899), 31. Christine Bold, "Popular Forms I," in Emory Elliot et al., eds., *The Columbia History of the American Novel* (New York: Columbia University Press, 1991), 285–305. Michael Denning emphasizes class conflict between working and managerial/owner classes in his *Mechanic Accents: Dime Novels and Working-Class Culture in America* (New York: Verso, 1987). Jones, *Dime Novel Western,* 81–89.

38. Warren French, "The Cowboy in the Dime Novel," *Texas Studies in English* 30 (1951): 219–34.

39. Jones, *Dime Novel Western,* 100–101; Joe B. Frantz and Julian Ernest Choate, Jr., *The American Cowboy: The Myth and Reality* (Norman: University of Oklahoma Press, 1955), 140–57.

40. Prentiss Ingraham, *Parson Jim, King of the Cowboys; or, the Gentle Shepherd's Big Clean Out* (1882), quoted in Mody C. Boatright, "The Beginnings of Cowboy Fiction," *Southwest Review* 51 (Winter 1966): 27; Frantz and Choate, *American Cowboy,* 147.

41. Prentiss Ingraham, *Buck Taylor, the Saddle King; or, The Lasso Rangers' League,* Beadle's Dime Library 50 (April 1, 1891): 2.

42. Ingraham, *The Cowboy Clan; or, The Tigress of Texas* (1891), quoted in Boatright, "Beginnings of Cowboy Fiction," 20.

43. William G. Patten, *Wild Vulcan the Lone Rider; or, the Rustlers of the Bad Lands, A Romance of Nebraska* (1890), and William West Wilder (William G. Patten), *Cowboy Chris, the Desert Centaur; or, Hawking the Human Hawk, a Story of the Arid Plains* (1897), quoted in ibid., 25.

44. For substantiation of this point on chronology, see the pertinent chapters in Steckmesser, *The Western Hero;* Glenn Shirley, *Belle Starr and Her Times: The Literature, The Facts, and The Legends* (Norman: University of Oklahoma Press, 1982), 3–28; Richard W. Etulain, "Calamity Jane: Independent Woman of the Wild West," in Glenda Riley and Richard W. Etulain, eds., *By Grit and Grace: Eleven Women Who Shaped the American West* (Golden, Colo.: Fulcrum Publishing, 1997), 72–92.

45. Mary Noel, *Villains Galore . . . The Heyday of the Popular Story Weekly* (New York: Macmillan Company, 1954).

46. For a thorough, up-to-date biography, see Allan G. Bogue, *Frederick Jackson Turner: Strange Roads Going Down* (Norman: University of Oklahoma Press, 1998). The following section on Turner draws on Richard W. Etulain, ed., *Does the Frontier Experience Make America Exceptional?* (Boston: Bedford Books, 1999), 3–14.

47. "Problems in American History," *Aegis* 7 (November 4, 1892): 48–52; reprinted in *The Early Writings of Frederick Jackson Turner* (Madison: University of Wisconsin, 1938), 71–83, quotes on pp. 72, 83.

48. The 1893 essay first appeared as Frederick J. Turner, "The Significance of the Frontier in American History," in *Annual Report of the American Historical Association for the Year 1893* (Washington: GPO and American Historical Association, 1894), 199–227, quotes on pp. 199, 226–27.

49. See Turner's letter to Constance Skinner, March 15, 1922, Box 31, Turner Papers, Henry E. Huntington Library, San Marino, California.

50. "Significance of the Frontier," 200.

51. Ibid., 223.

52. For an interpretation that differs from the discussion here of Turner and Buffalo Bill Cody, see Richard White, "Frederick Jackson Turner and Buffalo Bill"; and White, "When Frederick Jackson Turner and Buffalo Bill Both Played Chicago in 1893," in *Frontier and Region: Essays in Honor of Martin Ridge,* ed. Robert C. Ritchie and Paul Andrew Hutton (Albuquerque: University of New Mexico Press, 1997), 201–12.

Chapter Two: Untold Stories

1. Arnold Krupat provides a useful sampling of these Indian narratives in his edited collection *Native American Autobiography: An Anthology* (Madison: University of Wisconsin Press, 1994). For a helpful listing of Native lifestories, consult H. David Brumble III, *An Annotated Bibliography of American Indian and Eskimo Autobiographies* (Lincoln: University of Nebraska Press, 1981).

2. S. M. Barrett, ed., *Geronimo's Story of His Life* (New York: Duffield and Company, 1906).

3. Hum-ishu-ma ("Mourning Dove"), *Co=ge=we=a, The Half-Blood: A Depiction of the Great Montana Cattle Range* (Boston: Four Seas Company, 1927).

4. Rodman W. Paul, ed. *A Victorian Gentlewoman in the Far West: The Reminiscences of Mary Hallock Foote* (San Marino, Calif.: Huntington Library, 1972). A collection of more than five hundred of Foote's revealing letters and copies and originals of some of her art-work are in the Special Collections of the Stanford University Library.

5. See, for example, M. H. Foote to Helena de Kay Gilder, November 16, 1887, #318, Box 7, Folder 3, and Foote to Gilder, March 6, 1887, Box 7, Folder 2, Mary Hallock Foote Papers, Stanford.

6. The two most useful accounts of Foote's life and works are Lee Ann Johnson, *Mary Hallock Foote* (Boston: Twayne, 1980), and James H. Maguire, *Mary Hallock Foote* (Boise, Idaho: Boise State College, 1972).

7. Foote's shorter fiction and woodcut art are conveniently sampled in Barbara Cragg et al., eds., *The Idaho Stories and Far West Illustrations of Mary Hallock Foote* (Pocatello: Idaho State University, 1988).

8. Melody Graulich, "Profile of Mary Hallock Foote," *Legacy* 3 (No. 2, 1986): 43–52; Shelley Armitage, "The Illustrator as Writer: Mary Hallock Foote and the Myth of the West," in Barbara Howard Meldrum, ed., *Under the Sun: Myth and Realism in Western American Literature* (Troy, N.Y.: Whitston, 1985), 150–74.

9. Mary Hallock Foote, *The Led-Horse Claim: A Romance of a Mining Camp* (Boston: James R. Osgood and Company, 1883). Page references to this and subsequent works are within the text.

10. Foote, *The Last Assembly Ball: A Pseudo Romance of the Far West* (Boston: Houghton, Mifflin and Company, 1889).

11. A Victorian Gentlewoman, 265.

12. Foote, *The Last Assembly Ball,* 6.

13. Foote to Gilder, April 10, 1887, #314, Box 7, Folder 2, Foote Collection, Stanford.

14. Until someone completes the much-needed full-length study of Mary Hallock Foote as an important artist, we must rely on a brief discussion in Robert Taft, *Artists and Illustrators of the Old West, 1850–1900* (New York: Charles Scribner's Sons, 1953), Regina Armstrong, "Representative American Women Illustrators: The Character Workers," *Critic* 37 (August 1900): 131–41, and Barbara Cragg, "The Landscape Perceptions and Imagery of Mary Hallock Foote" (Master's thesis, University of Montana, 1980).

15. The Far West series is reprinted in Cragg, *The Idaho Stories,* 267–303. In-text page references are to this collection. Realistic, factual, and representational in form and content, these woodcut artworks also indicate how much Foote's views of the West differed from those of near contemporaries like Frederic Remington and Charles Russell.

16. "The Engineer's Mate" appeared as an illustration for William E. Smythe, "The Conquest of Arid America," *Century Magazine* 50 (May 1895): 90; *A Victorian Gentlewoman,* 275.

17. For especially supercilious comments about westerners and Idahoans specifically, see Foote to Gilder, May 19, 1883, #84, Box 6, Folder 32; April 4, 1885, #288, Box 6, Folder 37; June 12, 1891, Box 7, Folder 10, Foote Papers, Stanford.

18. *Between the Desert and the Sown* is reprinted in *A Victorian Gentlewoman,* 294.

19. This section on Calamity Jane draws heavily on the research contained in Richard W. Etulain, "Calamity Jane: Independent Woman of the Wild West," in Glenda Riley and Richard W. Etulain, eds., *By Grit and Grace: Eleven Women Who Made the American West* (Golden, Colo.: Fulcrum Publishers, 1997), 72–92.

20. The most reliable sources on Calamity Jane are Roberta Beed Sollid, *Calamity Jane: A Study in Historical Criticism* (1958; Helena: Montana Historical Society Press, 1995); James D. McLaird, "Calamity Jane: The Life and the Legend," *South Dakota History* 24 (Spring 1994): 1–18; McLaird, "Calamity Jane's Diary and Letters: Story of a Fraud," *Montana: The Magazine of Western History* 45 (Autumn-Winter 1995): 20–35; and McLaird, "Calamity Jane and Wild Bill: Myth and Reality," *Journal of the West* 37 (April 1998): 23–32.

21. Although it must be used with caution, Duncan Aikman's *Calamity Jane and the Lady Wildcats* (New York: H. Holt and Company, 1927) contains the most extensive comments on Martha Canary's earliest years. The U.S. Census of 1860, Mercer County, Missouri, lists the Canary family as residing in the Ravanna Township, near Princeton.

22. *Montana Post* (Virginia City), December 31, 1864.

23. Calamity Jane, *Life and Adventures of Calamity Jane by Herself* (N. p.: n. p., [1896?]). Special territorial census, 1869, Piedmont, Carter County, Wyoming.

24. Lesta V. Turchen and James D. McLaird, *The Black Hills Expedition of 1875* (Mitchell, S. D.: Dakota Wesleyan University Press, 1975); William B. Secrest, ed., *I Buried Hickok: Memoir of White Eye Anderson* (College Station, Tex.: Creative Publishing Company, 1980). Joseph F. ("White Eye") Anderson to C. M. Lawrence, January 28, 1943, Folder 9, Calamity Jane–Wild Bill Hickok Collection, Fort Collins Museum, Fort Collins, Colorado.

25. H. N. Maguire, *The Black Hills and American Wonderland: From Personal Explorations* (Chicago: Donnelley, Lloyd, 1877); Edward L. Wheeler, *Deadwood Dick, the Prince of the Road; or, The Black Rider of the Black Hills,* Beadle's Half-Dime Library, #1 (New York: Beadle and Adams, October 15, 1877): T. M. Newson, *Drama of Life in the Black Hills* (Saint Paul, Minn.: Dodge and Larpenteur, 1878). I am indebted to Professor James McLaird for calling my attention to Newson's play.

26. *Rocky Mountain News,* June 10, 1877, p. 3, col 4; Maguire, *The Black Hills,* 304.

27. Richard W. Etulain, "Calamity Jane: Creation of a Western Legend. An Afterword," in Sollid, *Calamity Jane* (1995), 149–63.

28. Several important newspaper stories about Calamity are collected in Nolie Mumey, *Calamity Jane, 1852–1903: A History of Her Life and Adventures in the West* (Denver: Range Press, 1950); Bill and Doris Whithorn, *Calamity's in Town: The Town was Livingston, Montana* (Livingston: Livingston Enterprises, 197?); and Stella Foote, *A History of Calamity Jane: Our Country's First Liberated Woman* (New York: Vantage Press, 1996).

29. Whithorn and Whithorn, *Calamity's in Town;* "'Calamity Jane': 'Buffalo Bill's' Recollections," *London Star,* August 7, 1903, Buffalo Bill Clipping Book, 1903, p. 78, Buffalo Bill Historical Center, Cody, Wyoming.

30. McLaird, "Calamity Jane: The Life and Legend"; E. C. Abbott ("Teddy Blue") and Helen Huntington Smith, *We Pointed Them North: Recollections of a Cowpuncher* (Norman: University of Oklahoma Press, 1954), 76; Teddy Blue [Abbott], "When I First Met Calamity Jane," in I. D. O'Donnell, *Montana Monographs,* Billings, Montana, Public Library, 1928–29.

31. Jean A. Mathisen, "Calamity's Sister," *True West* 43 (December 1996): 23–26, 28–30; Tobe Borner to Clarence S. Paine, March 23, 1945, Paine Collection, Center for Western Studies, Augustana College, Sioux Falls, S. D.

32. "'Calamity Jane's' Name Was Canary," *Park County News* (Livingston, Montana), June 16, 1922; Elijah Cannary [*sic*] file, #253, State Penitentiary Files, Wyoming State Archives, Cheyenne.

33. *Yellowstone Journal* (Miles City, Montana), November 25, 1882; *Cheyenne Daily Leader,* June 21, 1887, p. 3, col. 3.

34. McLaird, "Calamity Jane's Diary and Letters," thoroughly and persuasively dismisses the purported Calamity diary as a fraud.

35. Bingham County Records, Territory of Idaho, May 30, 1888, Idaho Historical Society, Boise.

36. *The Illustrated American*, March 7, 1896, 312. Reference courtesy James D. McLaird.

37. A large group of photographs of Calamity is printed in Foote, *A History of Calamity Jane,* 79–94, 161–76. Useful explanations of some of the best-known photographs of Calamity appear in J. Leonard Jennewein, *Calamity Jane of the Western Trails* (Rapid City, S. D.: Dakota West Books, 1953, 1991).

38. Etulain, "Calamity Jane: Creation of a Western Legend."

39. Three studies are exceptionally useful sources for understanding Native American autobiographies: Arnold Krupat, *For Those Who Come After: A Study of Native American Autobiography* (Berkeley: University of California Press, 1985); David H. Brumble III, *American Indian Autobiography* (Berkeley: University of California Press, 1988); Hertha Dawn Wong, *Sending My Heart Back Across the Years: Tradition and Innovation in Native American Autobiography* (New York: Oxford University Press, 1992).

40. Chief Joseph, "An Indian's Views of Indian Affairs," *North American Review* 128 (April 1879); Chief Joseph, *Chief Joseph's Own Story* (St Paul [?]: Great Northern Railway, 1925).

41. Barrett, ed., *Geronimo's Story of His Life,* xiii-xiv. Subsequent page references are within the text.

42. Krupat, *For Those Who Come After;* Frederick Turner, "Introduction," to Barrett, *Geronimo: His Own Life* (New York: Meridian Book, 1996). See Turner's footnote annotations throughout the volume.

43. Angie Debo, *Geronimo: The Man, His Time, His Place* (Norman: University of Oklahoma Press, 1976), 5.

44. C. L. Sonnichsen, "The Ambivalent Apache," *Western American Literature* 10 (August 1975): 99–114; C. L. Sonnichsen, "From Savage to Saint: A New Image for Geronimo," in Sonnichsen, ed. *Geronimo and the End of the Apache Wars* (Lincoln: University of Nebraska Press, 1990), 5–34.

45. Krupat, *For Those Who Come After.*

46. Mourning Dove (Hum-ishu-ma), *Cogewea, The Half-Blood* (1927; Lincoln: University of Nebraska Press, 1981), "Introduction" by Dexter Fisher. Recently, some scholars have promoted S. Alice Callahan's *Wynema: A Child of the Forest* (1891; Lincoln: University of Nebraska Press, 1997) as the first novel by an Indian woman.

47. The fullest account of Mourning Dove's life is contained in Jay Miller, ed., *Mourning Dove: A Salishan Autobiography* (Lincoln: University of Nebraska Press, 1990). See also Alice Poindexter Fisher, "The Transformation of Tradition: A Study of Zitkala-sa [Bonnin] and Mourning Dove, Two Transitional Indian Writers" (Ph. D. dissertation, City University of New York, 1979).

48. Mourning Dove gives scattered glimpses of her life in her letters to Lucullus Virgil McWhorter in the McWhorter Collection, Holland Library, Washington State University, Pullman, Washington. For a guide to this collection, see Nelson Alt, *The Papers of Lucullus Virgil McWhorter* (Pullman: Friends of the Washington State University, 1959).

49. Steven R. Evans, *Voice of the Old Wolf: Lucullus Virgil McWhorter and the Nez Perce Indians* (Pullman: Washington State University Press, 1996), 4, 56.

50. Evans, *Voice of the Old Wolf,* 56, 64. Mourning Dove to McWhorter, March 27, April 30, 1916; Mourning Dove to "Big Foot" [McWhorter], May 21, 1927, McWhorter Collection. "Colville Indian Girl Blazes Trail to New Conception of Redmen in Her Novel, 'Cogewea', Soon to Be Published," *The Spokesman Review* (Spokane, Washington), April 9, 1916.

51. Mourning Dove to McWhorter, September 4, 1916, McWhorter Collection.

52. Dexter Fisher, "Introduction," *Cogewea,* xxv.

53. Two writers who emphasize Mourning Dove's voice in *Cogewea* are Susan K. Bernardin, "Mixed Messages: Authority and Authorship in Mourning Dove's "*Cogewea, The Half-Blood: A Depiction of the Great Montana Cattle Range,*" *American Literature* 67 (September 1995): 487–509; and Alanna Kathleen Brown, "Mourning Dove's Voice in *Cogewea,*" *Wicazo Sa Review* 4 (Spring 1988): 2–15.

54. McWhorter to Dr. McLean, January 3, May 18, 1916; McWhorter to Joseph Latimer, August 25, 1924; McWhorter to Mourning Dove [with her annotations], February 20, 1916, McWhorter Collection.

55. Mourning Dove to "Big Foot," June 4, 1928, McWhorter Collection.

56. Mourning Dove to McWhorter, May 14, September 4, 1916; November 10, 1926, McWhorter Collection.

Chapter Three: Traditional Stories

1. Owen Wister to "Dearest Mother," July 5, 1902, *Owen Wister Out West: His Journals and Letters,* ed. Fanny Kemble Wister (Chicago: University of Chicago Press, 1958), 17–18.

2. Darwin Payne provides the best biographical source on Wister in *Owen Wister: Chronicler of the West, Gentleman of the East* (Dallas: Southern Methodist University Press, 1985). See also G. Edward White, *The Eastern Establishment and the Western Experience: The West of Frederic Remington, Theodore Roosevelt, and Owen Wister* (New Haven: Yale University Press, 1968), and Richard W. Etulain, *Owen Wister* (Boise, Idaho: Boise State University, 1973).

3. Owen Wister, *The Virginian: The Horseman of the Plains* (New York: Macmillan, 1902), 4, 5. Subsequent page references within the text are to this edition.

4. John L. Cobbs, *Owen Wister* (Boston: Twayne Publishers, 1984), 84.

5. Wister, "Re-dedication and Preface," *The Virginian* (New York: Macmillan, 1911), n. p.

6. *Owen Wister Out West: His Journals and Letters,* 112.

7. For interesting comments on Wister's greenhorn narrator, see Sanford E. Marovitz, "Testament of a Patriot: The Virginian, the Tenderfoot, and Owen Wister," *Texas Studies in Language and Literature* 15 (Fall 1973): 551–75.

8. John Seelye, "Introduction," to Owen Wister, *The Virginian: A Horseman of the Plains* (New York: Penguin Books, 1988), xxiv-xxv, xxxii–xxxiii.

9. Owen Wister, *Members of the Family* (New York: Macmillan, 1911), 5.

10. For a reading of *The Virginian* that disagrees with most of the observations presented here, see Lee Clark Mitchell, *Westerns: Making the Man in Fiction and Film* (Chicago: University of Chicago Press, 1996), 94–119. Jane Tompkins provocatively rereads the role of Molly Wood and comes to controversial conclusions in *West of Everything: The Inner Life of Westerns* (New York: Oxford Unversity Press, 1992), 141–43, 149–50. For a revisionist reading of the place of *The Virginian* in Wister's career, see Louis Tanner, "Owen Wister: The Public Intellectual" (Ph.D. dissertation, University of New Mexico, 1999).

11. Wister, "How Lin McLean Went East," *Harper's Magazine* 86 (December 1892): 135; Wister, "The Evolution of the Cow-Puncher," *Harper's Magazine* 91 (September 1895): 615; Wister to Remington, August 25, 1895, quoted in Ben Merchant Vorpahl, *My Dear Wister: The Frederic Remington-Owen Wister Letters* (Palo Alto, Calif.: American West Publishing Company, 1972), 75.

12. Walter Noble Burns, *The Saga of Billy the Kid* (Garden City, N.Y.: Doubleday, Page & Company, 1926).

13. Frederick Nolan provides a capsule discussion of the career of Walter Noble Burns in his new book, *The West of Billy the Kid* (Norman: University of Oklahoma Press, 1998), 295–98. For other comments on Burns's influential role in the interpretations of Billy the Kid, see Stephen Tatum, *Inventing Billy the Kid: Visions of the Outlaw in America, 1881–1981* (Albuquerque: University of New Mexico Press, 1982). Tatum writes that Burns's *Saga* "has generated more controversy than any other book in the Kid's bibliography" (102). W. A. Carrell to Maurice Garland Fulton, April 20 [?], 1929, Maurice Garland Fulton Papers, Box 1, Folder 6, University of Arizona Library, Tucson.

14. Carrell to Fulton, February 12, 1930, Box 1, Folder 6, Fulton Papers.

15. "Confessions," *Chicago Daily Tribune,* May 8, 1926.

16. Carrell to Fulton, February 12, 1930.

17. Mrs. Susan E. Barber to Maurice Fulton, December 22, 1925; Barber to Fulton, March 24, 1926; Barber to Fulton, May 18, 1930, Fulton Papers, Box 1, Folder 4.

18. Susan E. Barber to Walter Noble Burns, November 21, 1928, Walter Noble Burns Papers, Box 1, University of Arizona Library, Tucson.

19. Walter Noble Burns to Maurice Garland Fulton, January 21 [1926], M. G. Fulton Papers, Box 1, Folder 2; Burns to My Dear Mrs. Barber, February 18 [1926], Fulton Papers, Box 1, Folder 4.

20. Burns to Mrs. Barber, February 18 [1926]; W. A. Carrell to M. G. Fulton, April 20 [?], 1929, February 12, 1930, Box 1, Folder 6, Garland Papers.

21. Richard Maxwell Brown, *No Duty to Retreat: Violence and Values in American History and Society* (New York: Oxford University Press, 1992).

22. Walter Noble Burns to Barrett Kiesling (Metro-Goldwyn-Mayer Studios), May 22, 1930, Walter Noble Burns Papers, Box 1, Folder 1.

23. The most useful overviews of the film Western are George N. Fenin and William Everson, *The Western: From Silents to the Seventies,* rev. ed. (New York: Grossman, 1973), and Jon Tuska, *The Filming of the West* (Garden City, N.Y.: Doubleday, 1976). Portions of the following paragraphs appeared earlier in Richard W. Etulain, "Changing Images: The Cowboy in Western Films," *Colorado Heritage* 1 (No. 1, 1981): 37–55.

24. John G. Cawelti, *Adventure, Mystery, and Romance: Formula Stories as Art and Popular Culture* (Chicago: University of Chicago Press, 1976), 230–41. Jon Tuska often dissents from Cawelti's views and those of most other American Studies scholars. See especially, Jon Tuska and Vicki Piekarski, eds., *The Frontier Experience: A Reader's Guide to the Life and Literature of the American West* (Jefferson, N.C.: McFarland, 1984), 310, 317, 318–19.

25. Lary May, *Screening Out the Past: The Birth of Mass Culture and the Motion Picture Industry* (Chicago: University of Chicago Press, 1980), 257. The best reference guide to the film Western is Edward Buscombe, ed. *The BFI Companion to the Western* (New York: Atheneum, 1988).

26. Ernest Haycox, "Stage to Lordsburg," *Collier's* (April 10, 1937), reprinted in *The Best Western Stories of Ernest Haycox* (New York: Bantam Books, 1960), 123–36; "John Ford on *Stagecoach*" in Richard J. Anobile, ed., *John Ford's Stagecoach Starring John Wayne* (New York: Avon/Flare Books, 1975), 6–7.

27. "John Ford on *Stagecoach,*" 6. The volume edited by Anobile contains 250 pages of stills from *Stagecoach.* For another useful casebook on *Stagecoach,* see Edward Buscombe, *Stagecoach* (London: BFI Pub., 1992).

28. For two recent studies of Ford and his cinematic artistry, see Tag Gallagher, *John Ford: The Man and His Films* (Berkeley: University of California Press, 1986), and Ronald L. Davis, *John Ford: Hollywood's Old Master* (Norman: University of Oklahoma Press, 1995).

29. I have learned much about John Wayne from Randy Roberts and James S. Olson,

John Wayne American (New York: The Free Press, 1995), and Garry Wills, *John Wayne's America: The Politics of Celebrity* (New York: Simon & Schuster, 1997).

30. Robert L. Gale, *Louis L'Amour* (Boston: Twayne Publishers, 1985), 12. In addition to Gale's very useful overview, those interested in L'Amour should consult Robert Weinberg, *The Louis L'Amour Companion* (Kansas City, Missouri: Andrews and McMeel, 1992), and Candace Klaschus, "Louis L'Amour: The Writer as Teacher" (Ph.D. dissertation, University of New Mexico, 1983). The latter source is particularly valuable for the several interviews with L'Amour from which that author quotes.

31. Louis L'Amour, "The Gift of Cochise," *Collier's* (July 5, 1952); L'Amour, *Hondo* (New York: Fawcett-Gold Medal Books, 1953). Jon Tuska, "Hondo—Novel or Novelization," in Weinberg, 211–12; Scott A. Cupp, "Hondo Lane and Louis L'Amour," in Weinberg, 208–10.

32. Klaschus, "Louis L'Amour," 46. L'Amour adds other information about his story-telling in Michael T. Marsden, "A Conversation with Louis L'Amour," *Journal of American Culture* 2 (Winter 1980): 646–58.

33. John D. Nesbitt provides helpful comment on *Hondo* in "A New Look at Two Popular Western Classics," *South Dakota Review* 18 (Spring 1980): 30–42. See also Nesbitt, "Change of Purpose in the Novels of Louis L'Amour," *Western American Literature* 13 (Spring 1978): 65–81.

34. Louis L'Amour, *The Sackett Companion: A Personal Guide to the Sackett Novels* (New York: Bantam, 1988), 10. For a brief overview of L'Amour's family saga novels, consult Michael T. Marsden, "The Concept of Family in the Fiction of Louis L'Amour," *North Dakota Quarterly* 46 (Summer 1978): 12–21.

35. Louis L'Amour, *Bendigo Shafter* (New York: Bantam, 1979). John Nesbitt, "Louis L'Amour—Paper Mâché Homer?" *South Dakota Review* 19 (Autumn 1981): 39.

36. Marsden, "Concept of Family," 12–16.

37. Louis L'Amour to B. A. Botkin, February 28, 1934, Regionalism box, B. A. Botkin Papers, University of Nebraska Archives, Love Library, University of Nebraska-Lincoln. Louis L'Amour to Richard W. Etulain, March 15, 1982.

38. Chungkham Sheela Ramani, "Women in the American West: A Study of the Role of Women in the Major Novels of Louis L'Amour" (Ph.D. dissertation, Manipur University [India], 1996).

39. As Robert Gale points out, "an entire monograph could be written on L'Amour and the Indian." *Louis L'Amour,* 113.

40. For an abbreviated discussion of L'Amour's efforts to experiment with several fictional genres, consult R. Jeff Banks, "The Mix-Master—L'Amour's Crossover Novels," in Weinberg, 235–41.

41. "The Homer of the Oater," *Time* 116 (December 1, 1980): 107–8.

42. Louis L'Amour, *The High Graders* (New York: Bantam, 1965), 70.

Chapter Four: New Stories

1. We lack a study of humor in western film and fiction. For a brief discussion of satires and parodies in cinematic Westerns, see George N. Fenin and William K. Everson, *The Western: From Silents to the Seventies,* rev ed. (New York: Penguin Books, 1977), 253–54 passim. C. L. Sonnichsen provided a useful anthology of humorous western writing and helpful editorial comment in *The Laughing West: Humorous Western Fiction Past and Present: An Anthology* (Athens: Swallow Press/Ohio University Press, 1980.)

2. The most helpful study of regionalism in the American West and American South is Robert L. Dorman, *Revolt of the Provinces: The Regionalist Movement in America, 1920–1945* (Chapel Hill: University of North Carolina Press, 1993). Western subregional identities are treated in a valuable collection of essays edited by David M. Wrobel and Michael C. Steiner, *Many Wests: Place, Culture, & Regional Identity* (Lawrence: University Press of Kansas, 1997).

3. The two most extensive overviews of western American literature are contained in J. Golden Taylor and Thomas J. Lyon, et al., eds., *A Literary History of the American West* (Fort Worth: Texas Christian University Press, 1987), and Western Literature Association, *Updating the Literary West* (Fort Worth: Texas Christian University Press, 1997).

4. Wallace Stegner, *Angle of Repose* (Garden City, N.Y.: Doubleday, 1971). Jackson J. Benson provides a wonderfully positive biography of Stegner in *Wallace Stegner: His Life and Work* (New York: Viking, 1996). A near-exhaustive listing of Stegner's works appears in Nancy Colberg, *Wallace Stegner: A Descriptive Bibliography* (Lewiston, Idaho: Confluence Press, 1990).

5. Wallace Stegner and Richard W. Etulain, *Stegner: Conversations on History and Literature* (1983; Reno: University of Nevada Press, 1996). These pages on Stegner draw heavily on Richard W. Etulain, "Wallace Stegner: Western Humanist," *Montana: The Magazine of Western History* 43 (Autumn 1993): 74–76; and Etulain, "Western Fiction and History: A Reconsideration," in Jerome E. Steffen, ed., *The American West: New Perspectives, New Dimensions* (Norman: University of Oklahoma Press, 1979), 152–74.

6. Stegner wrote his "Wilderness Letter" in 1960 to David E. Pesonen at the Agricultural Experiment Station at the University of California. The letter appears in Stegner, *The Sound of Mountain Water* (New York: E. P. Dutton, 1980), and is widely reprinted. For recent discussions of Stegner as a conservationist and environmentalist, see Page Stegner and Mary Stegner, eds., *The Geography of Hope: A Tribute to Wallace Stegner* (San Francisco: Sierra Books, 1996), and Curt Meine, ed., *Wallace Stegner and the Continental Vision: Essays on Literature, History, and Landscape* (Washington, D.C.: Island Press, 1997).

7. Curiously, *Angle of Repose* never received a full review in the *New York Times Review.* Neither did *The Spectator Bird* (1976), which won a National Book Award. See Stegner's comments on these oversights in *Conversations,* 14, 96–97.

8. The fullest discussion of western historiographical trends appears in Gerald D. Nash, *Creating the West: Historical Interpretations 1890–1990* (Albuquerque: University of New Mexico Press, 1991).

9. The extent to which Stegner draws on the life and writings of Mary Hallock Foote can be traced in Rodman W. Paul, ed., *A Victorian Gentlewoman in the Far West: The Reminiscences of Mary Hollock Foote* (San Marino, Calif.: Huntington Library, 1972), and in Lee Ann Johnson *Mary Hallock Foote* (Boston: Twayne Publishers, 1980).

10. Bernard DeVoto, "The West: A Plundered Province," *Harper's Magazine* 169 (August 1934): 355–64.

11. Henry Nash Smith, *Virgin Land: The American West as Symbol and Myth* (Cambridge, Mass.: Harvard University Press, 1950); Earl Pomeroy, "Toward a Reorientation of Western History: Continuity and Environment," *Mississippi Valley Historical Review* 41 (March 1955): 579–600, and Pomeroy, *The Pacific Slope: A History of California, Oregon, Washington, Idaho, Utah, and Nevada* (New York: Knopf, 1965).

12. Quoted in the *Salt Lake Tribune,* June 11, 1972.

13. John R. Milton, "Conversation with Wallace Stegner," *South Dakota Review* 9 (Spring 1971): 53, 54.

14. Richard W. Etulain, "Stegner the Novelist," Paper for the 34th Annual Conference, Western History Association, Albuquerque, N.M., October 23, 1994, quoted in Stewart L. Udall, "Foreword to the Nevada Edition," *Conversations,* vi.

15. For the sharpest criticism of Stegner's use of the Foote materials, see Mary Ellen Williams Walsh, "*Angle of Repose* and the Writings of Mary Hallock Foote: A Source Study," in Anthony Arthur, ed., *Critical Essays on Wallace Stegner* (Boston: G. K. Hall, 1982), 184–209; and David Lavender, "The Tyranny of Facts," in Judy Nolte Lensink, ed., *Old Southwest/New Southwest: Essays on a Region and Its Literature* (Tucson: Tucson Public Library, 1987), 68–73. Stegner defends his uses of Foote's life and letters in *Angle of Repose* in *Conversations,* 83–100; so does Jackson Benson in *Wallace Stegner,* 351–56.

16. Crow Indian scholar and writer Elizabeth Cook-Lynn castigates Stegner for what she considers his oversights and mistakes in treating Indian culture, especially in the title essay of her collection, *Why I Can't Read Wallace Stegner and Other Essays: A Tribal Voice* (Madison: University of Wisconsin Press, 1996). For a probing evaluation of this volume and Stegner's treatment of Indian topics, see the review of Cook-Lynn's volume by C. L. Rawlins, *Western American Literature* 32 (November 1997): 291–96.

17. For two especially valuable essays on the achievements of *Angle of Repose,* consult Melody Graulich, "'The Guides to Conduct That a Tradition Offers': Wallace Stegner's *Angle of Repose,*" *South Dakota Review* 23 (Winter 1985): 87–106, and Graulich, "Book Learning: *Angle of Repose* as Literary History," in Charles E. Rankin, ed., *Wallace Stegner: Man & Writer* (Albuquerque: University of New Mexico Press, 1996), 231–53.

18. Recent trends in western historiography are covered in Gerald D. Nash, *Creating the West,* and Richard W. Etulain, ed., *Writing Western History: Essays on Major Western Historians* (Albuquerque: University of New Mexico Press, 1991), esp. 335–58. See also the collected essays and comments in Clyde A. Milner II, ed., *A New Significance: Re-envisioning the History of the American West* (New York: Oxford University Press, 1996), particularly Allan G. Bogue, "The Course of Western History's First Century," 3–28.

19. Charles S. Peterson provides an excellent brief overview of western historical writing in his essay, "Speaking for the Past," in Clyde A. Milner II, Carol A. O'Connor, and Martha A. Sandweiss, eds., *The Oxford History of the American West* (New York: Oxford University Press, 1994), 743–69. Also, consult the appropriate essays on ethnic, gender, and environmental subjects in William Cronon, George A. Miles, and Jay Gitlin, eds., *Under an Open Sky: Rethinking America's Western Past* (New York: W. W. Norton, 1992).

20. Patricia Nelson Limerick, *The Legacy of Conquest: The Unbroken Past of the American West* (New York: W. W. Norton, 1987).

21. Professor Limerick provides a valuable and entertaining introduction to her beginnings as a historian in a lecture entitled "Just in Time: Getting Reacquainted with the Real Western Heroes," Calvin Horn Lectures, University of New Mexico, November 1, 1995. For general comments about and reactions to Limerick and to her most important book, see Donald Worster et al., *"The Legacy of Conquest,* by Patricia Nelson Limerick: A Panel of Appraisal," *Western Historical Quarterly* 20 (August 1989): 303–22; and Daniel Tyler, "Barbecuing a 'Paleo-Liberal' . . .," *Gateway Heritage* 9 (Winter 1988–89): 38–42.

22. One of the few analyses of the structure and content of *The Legacy of Conquest* appears in Robert F. Berkhofer, *Beyond the Great Story: History and Text and Discourse* (Cambridge, Mass.: Belknap Press of Harvard University Press, 1995). But see also the collected essays in Forrest G. Robinson, ed., "The New Western History: An Assessment," *Arizona Quarterly* 53 (Summer 1997).

23. The fullest, recent account of the troubled life of Narcissa Whitman appears in Julie Roy Jeffrey, *Converting the West: A Biography of Narcissa Whitman* (Norman: University of Oklahoma Press, 1991).

24. The one-page manifesto, written in response to the present writer's query about the definition of the New Western history, appears in Patricia Nelson Limerick, "What on Earth Is the New Western History?" *Montana: The Magazine of Western History* 40 (Summer 1990): 61–64. For a handy collection of essays illustrating the New Western history, as well as commentaries on this recent approach, consult Patricia Nelson Limerick, Clyde A. Milner II, and Charles A. Rankin, eds., *Trails: Toward a New Western History* (Lawrence: University Press of Kansas, 1991).

25. Richard White, *"It's Your Misfortune and None of My Own": A New History of the American West* (Norman: University of Oklahoma Press, 1991).

26. Richard White, *The Roots of Dependency: Subsistence, Environment, and Social Change Among the Choctaws, Pawnees, and Navajos* (Lincoln: University of Nebraska Press, 1983); White, *The Middle Ground: Indians, Empires, and Republics in the Great Lakes Region, 1650–1815* (New York: Cambridge University Press, 1991).

27. William W. Savage, Jr., "The New Western History: Youngest Whore on the Block," *A B Bookman's Weekly* 92 (October 4, 1993): 1242–47.

28. William H. Goetzmann, "Crisis of the New—West?" *Continuity* 17 (Fall 1993): 30.

29. Gerald Thompson, "The New Western History: A Critical Analysis," *Continuity* 17 (Fall 1993): 6.

30. See the editor's introduction and essays by Gerald Thompson and Gerald D. Nash,

for example, in Gene M. Gressley, ed., *Old West/New West: Quo Vadis?* (Worland, Wyo.: High Plains Publishing, 1994).

31. Quoted in Janny Scott, "Rival Old West Historians Try to Put Own Brand on Frontier," *New York Times,* May 18, 1993, p. 5; and "Showdown in the New West," *Denver Post Magazine,* March 21, 1993, p. 7; and Richard Bernstein, "Unsettling the Old West," *New York Times Magazine,* March 18, 1990, 34, 56–59.

32. See, for instance, the essays collected in *A New Significance.*

33. The essays in Eric Foner, ed., *The New American History,* rev., exp. ed. (Philadelphia: Temple University Press, 1997), illustrate parallels between U.S. and western American historiography.

34. The overviews noted in note 2 provide helpful discussion of recent trends in western American literature. The major essays and books dealing with more than three hundred western authors are listed in Richard W. Etulain and N. Jill Howard, eds., *A Biographical Guide to the Study of Western American Literature,* 2d ed. (Albuquerque: University of New Mexico Press, 1995).

35. Leslie Marmon Silko, *Ceremony* (New York: Viking Press, 1977).

36. Biographical information on Silko is available in Per Seyersted, *Leslie Marmon Silko* (Boise, Idaho: Boise State University, 1980), and Kathleen M. Sands, ed., "A Special Symposium Issue on Leslie Marmon Silko's *Ceremony,*" *American Indian Quarterly* 5 (February 1979): 1–75.

37. The most useful books analyzing Native American writing as well as sources by Indians themselves are listed in Etulain and Howard, *A Biographical Guide,* 96–108.

38. Louis Owens, *Other Destinies: Understanding the American Indian Novel* (Norman: University of Oklahoma Press, 1992), 168–69.

39. Seyersted, *Silko,* 29.

40. Alan R. Velie, *Four American Indian Literary Masters: N. Scott Momaday, James Welch, Leslie Marmon Silko, and Gerald Vizenor* (Norman: University of Oklahoma Press, 1982), 105–21.

41. Quoted in Seyersted, *Silko,* 26.

42. Anne Wright, ed., *The Delicacy of Strength and Lace: Letters Between Leslie Marmon Silko and James Wright* (St. Paul, Minn.: Greywolf Press, 1986), 68.

43. Paula Gunn Allen, "The Feminine Landscape of Leslie Marmon Silko's *Ceremony,*" in Paula Gunn Allen, ed., *Studies in American Indian Literature: Critical Essays and Course Designs* (New York: Modern Language Association, 1983), 127–33; quotes on 127, 133.

44. A pioneering work on McMurtry is Charles D. Peavy, *Larry McMurtry* (Boston: Twayne, 1977). Clay Reynolds has edited the most extensive collection of essays in *Taking Stock: A Larry McMurtry Casebook* (Dallas: Southern Methodist University Press, 1989), which includes an extensive bibliography. Of the book-length studies of McMurtry, I have learned much from Mark Busby, *Larry McMurtry and the West: An Ambivalent Relationship* (Denton: University of North Texas Press, 1995).

45. Larry McMurtry, "The American Southwest: Cradle of Literary Art," quoted in Busby, *McMurtry and the West,* 5–6.

46. Larry McMurtry, *Horseman, Pass By* (New York: Harper, 1961).

47. Larry McMurtry, *Lonesome Dove* (New York: Simon and Schuster, 1985).

48. Larry McMurtry, "How the West Was Won or Lost," *New Republic* 203 (October 22, 1990): 36,37.

49. Patrick Bennett, "Larry McMurtry: Thalia, Houston, and Hollywood," *Talking with Texas Writers: Twelve Interviews* (College Station: Texas A & M University Press, 1980), 23–24. Also see the interview by Mervyn Rothstein, "A Texan Who Likes to Deflate the Legends of the Golden West," *New York Times,* November 1, 1988, C17ff.

50. Mark Busby summarizes some of the historical sources McMurtry utilized in *Lonesome Dove* in *McMurtry and the West,* 36–40. McMurtry's historical sources are also discussed in Don Graham, "*Lonesome Dove:* Butch and Sundance Go On a Cattledrive," *Southwestern American Literature* 12 (No. 1, 1986): 7–12.

51. Critics who single out McMurtry's superb creation in Lorena include Robert M. Adams, "The Bard of Wichita Falls," *New York Review of Books,* August 13, 1987, 39–41; and Ernestine P. Sewell, "McMurtry's Cowboy-God in *Lonesome Dove,*" *Western American Literature* 21 (November 1986): 219–25. Both essays are reprinted in *Taking Stock.*

52. Larry McMurtry, *In a Narrow Grave: Essays on Texas* (1968; New York: Simon and Schuster, 1989), 54. McMurtry also writes: "My first concern has commonly been with textures, not structures; with motions, rather than methods" (142).

53. Richard W. Etulain, *Re-imagining the Modern American West: A Century of Fiction, History, and Art* (Tucson: University of Arizona Press, 1996), 159.

54. Larry McMurtry, *Anything for Billy* (New York: Simon and Schuster, 1988); Larry McMurtry, *Buffalo Girls* (New York: Simon and Schuster, 1990).

Epilogue: Toward a New Gray Story

1. For an entertaining, well-written overview of recent representations of the American West in history, literature, and movies, as well as in music and dress, see Michael L. Johnson, *New Westers: The West in Contemporary American Culture* (Lawrence: University Press of Kansas, 1996).

2. Richard White, *New York Times Book Review* 103 (May 17, 1998): 39.

Index

Boldface numerals indicate an extended treatment of the subject.

Index

Index

Index